W9-BMI-031

Isometric Perspective

From Baby Blocks to
Dimensional Design in Quilts

by

Katie Pasquini-Masopust

Acknowledgments

I would like to thank the following people for all of their help and support:

Daye Calvert, who responded to my cries for computer help, and for getting the isometric graph into my machine;
my husband Bobby, for showing me a new dimension of patience and understanding;
Jessica, Bobby III, and Brad, for accepting me and allowing me to call them my kids;
Barbara, for her strength;
Bob Sr., "for being my Daddy";
Randi Loft Perkins, who lovingly corrects me;
J. W. Eaves, for my western-style studio and his helping hand;
Carole Smith, for getting me here, there, and everywhere;
Sherry Bradley, for introducing us to everyone;
Willie Watkins, for his hysterical stories;
Robert Hutwöhl, for making my computer a friend rather than an enemy;
Second Gear, for taking me on slow, contemplative rides;
Margarite Wilson and Irene Strege for testing the pattern on such short notice;
all of my students who listened, then created and got their pieces to me on time.

Photography by Peter Stazione, unless otherwise noted

Drawings by Katie Pasquini-Masopust

Editing by Randi Loft Perkins

Technical editing by Elizabeth Aneloski

Book design by Katie Pasquini-Masopust and Virginia Coull

Published by
C & T Publishing
P.O. Box 1456
Lafayette, California 94549

ISBN 0-914881-46-9

Library of Congress Catalog Card Number: 92-53798

Printed in the United States of America

Pasquini-Masopust, Katie.
    Isometric perspective / Katie Pasquini-Masopust.
      p.   cm.
    Includes bibliographical references.
    ISBN 0-914881-46-9 : $15.95
    1. Quilts—Patterns. 2. Color in textile crafts. 3. Isometric
projection. 4. Visual perception. I. Title.
NK9104.P38   1992
746.9 ' 7—dc20   92-53798
                                   CIP

10 9 8 7 6 5 4 3 2 1

To
Debra Ward,
a most courageous woman,
&
Eloise Buckner,
for opening doors to health

Foreword

It seems that I write a book every two years or so. In 1983, I self-published *Mandala,* my first book about designing modern wall hangings. In 1985, I self-published a beginner's book, entitled *Contemporary Sampler*, for those who wanted to get a different look with their traditional quilts. *3 Dimensional Design* was published in 1988. This time, I had an established publisher! Earlier that year, C & T Publishing bought the rights to my first two books and my self-publishing days were over. Hallelujah! Life is much simpler without having to deal with advertising, billing, orders, etc. Now it's 1992—too long a lapse since my last book, and I'm ready for another.

My interest in isometric perspective began when I ordered a book from Dover Publications, *Isometric Perspective Designs and How to Create Them.* There were many wonderful designs throughout the book. I combined a few of my favorites to create my first isometric quilt, *Labyrinth.* The background of this quilt is all hand pieced! That came from "moi," who said, "Machine piecing is the only way I will ever work; I hate to hand piece." I was in transit between homes (getting married to a wonderful man), and my studio was in boxes. I couldn't be without fabric in my hand so, before I put all of those wonderful fabrics into boxes, I cut many pieces and spent several months relaxing and hand piecing the hours away. I loved it. It took a year to finally complete *Labyrinth*; that is the longest it has ever taken me to finish a piece. The next step was to make some small, quick reward pieces; the small Iso's pieces were created. I then developed the Holes and Poles patterns and really enjoyed using the reverse appliqué in their construction. I began teaching isometrics as a class, barely keeping one step ahead of my students as we all learned and explored together. I have put all of the information together in this book so that you might enjoy creating isometric quilts as well.

I have included many pattern ideas in this book. These ideas can be combined with others or used alone. It is exciting to realize that Baby Blocks is isometric in the same way that the cover quilt, *Dimensional Portal*, is isometric.

I have a new name now, as you must have noticed, and a new life with a husband who is very supportive. I still teach and lecture throughout the U.S. and abroad, but not as often. I'm enjoying my new studio, staying home with my new family—and learning to ride horses!

Table of Contents

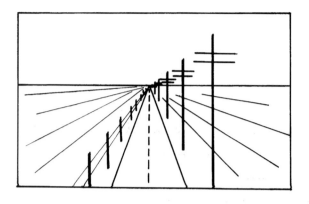

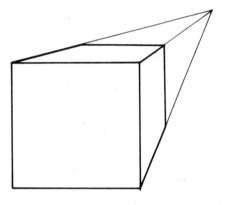

Isometric Perspective

There is a difference between isometric perspective and three-dimensional perspective. In three-dimensional perspective, a vanishing point is used and things are drawn to duplicate our perceptions: a road seems to narrow in the distance, parallel lines converge on the horizon, the sides of a box narrow in the distance.

In isometrics, the rules of composition are broken and all parallel lines remain parallel, creating an optical illusion of dimension. Draftsmen use isometrics to draw schematics of machinery and buildings. Each line is drawn to scale so the builder can construct the object drawn; no vanishing point is used.

Using isometric graph paper, you can create many designs. One of the oldest isometric quilt patterns is Baby Blocks; it is based on the isometric diamond. This pattern is achieved by putting together three isometric diamonds to create the illusion of a box. The dimension is enhanced by using light, medium, and dark colors.

The basic block can be changed in any number of ways to create more intricate patterns.

Isometric designs consist of the most basic Baby Blocks (color plate 1), to the more complicated Isos's (color plates 11 and 12), on to even more intricate designs as seen in *Dimensional Portal* (color plate 6) and *My Secret Garden* (color plate 8).

Tools

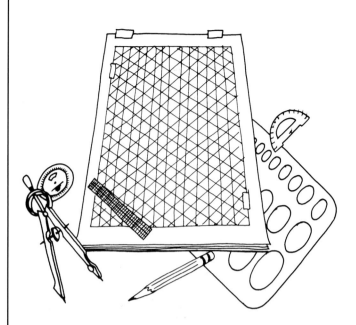

Isometric Graph Paper: This is available in tablets at art supply stores and some quilt shops. There is a piece of graph paper on the first page of this book. By placing tracing paper over the graph paper and tracing the lines needed, you can use this paper over and over. Do not photocopy this graph paper, because photocopy machines can distort the grid and inaccuracies may occur.

Ruler: Use a 6" grid ruler. It is small and easy to swing around when you are drawing different angles.

Tracing Paper: Any size will work.

Pencils: Any pencil is good as long as it is kept sharp.

Compass: A bow compass with a rotating adjustment wheel is best.

Protractor: Use the one with an "x" indicating the center.

Proportional Scale: This is used to reduce or enlarge the patterns.

Isometric Ellipse Guide: This template has isometric holes in varying sizes and is necessary for drawing ellipses. It is available at most art supply stores.

Reducing Tool: Binoculars, a reducing glass or a door peephole work well.

Draftsman's Tape: Available at art supply stores; used to secure tracing paper over graph paper.

Template Material: Use the unlined, frosted plastic.

Freezer Paper: Find this at the grocery store; it is used for reverse appliqué.

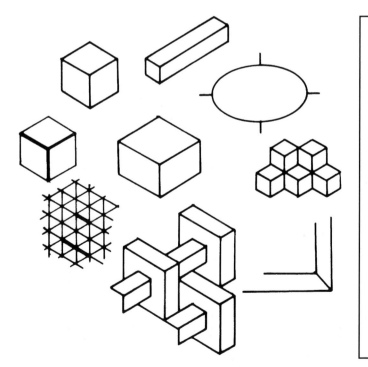

Terms

Block: A block consists of three isometric diamonds.

Cap: The completion of the ends of a beam or pole.

Ellipse References

    Vertical: The marks at the top and bottom of the ellipse opening, marking the vertical centers.

    Horizontal: The marks at the left and right side of the ellipse opening, marking the horizontal centers.

Group: Placing blocks with shared sides together.

Interlocking: Blocks whose irregular sides fit together.

Miter: Folding or sewing fabric together at a 45° angle.

Naked Block: A Baby Block with no divisions other than the center Y.

Thickness: The width of a slice.

Unit: The side of one triangle on the isometric graph paper.

Y point of view: A point of reference that is centered at the inside Y lines within each block.

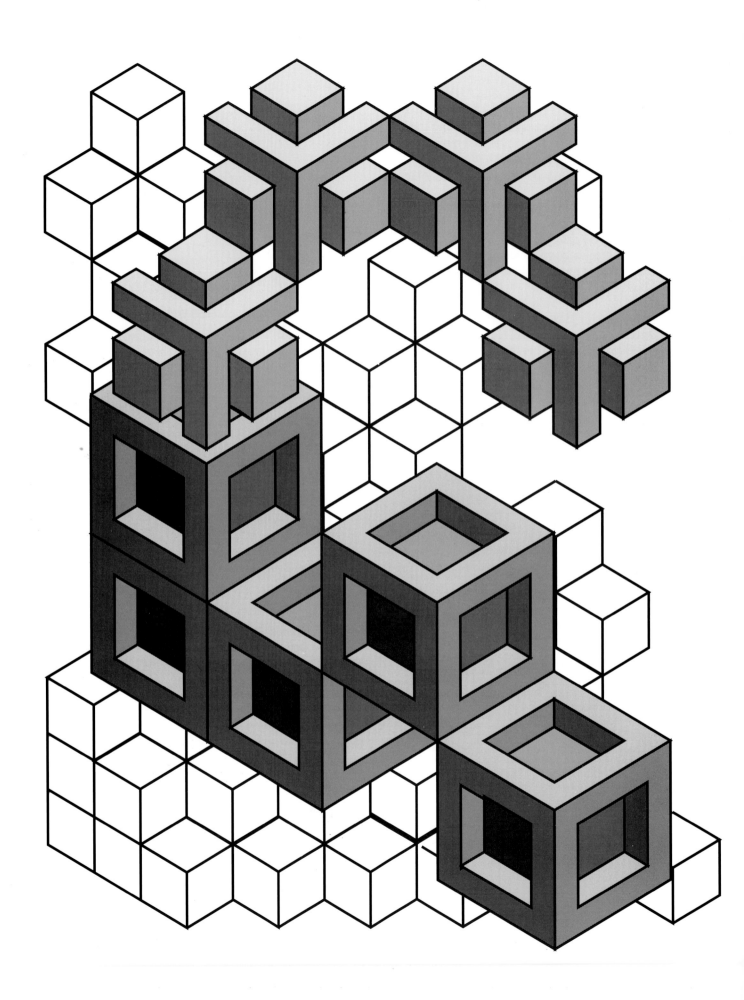

Baby Blocks

The basis for all the designs in this book is the Baby Block.

1. Begin by drawing the Baby Block using 2 units per side.

2. Draw several baby blocks, 2 units per side. They should be grouped side to side, creating an all-over pattern. This is a very basic first step, but it will help you to see how the blocks fit together.

These basic angles will be used again and again throughout the book. This shape is the 60° diamond. The two small angles are 60° and the two large angles are 120°.

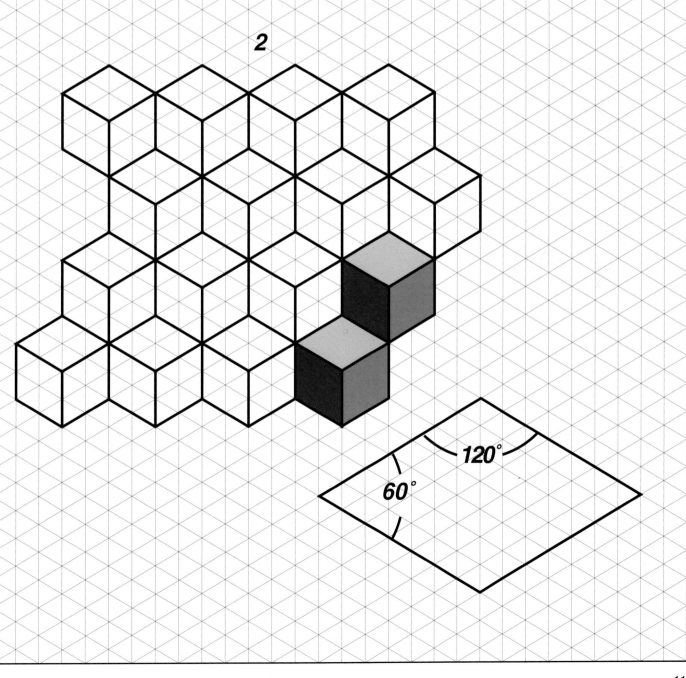

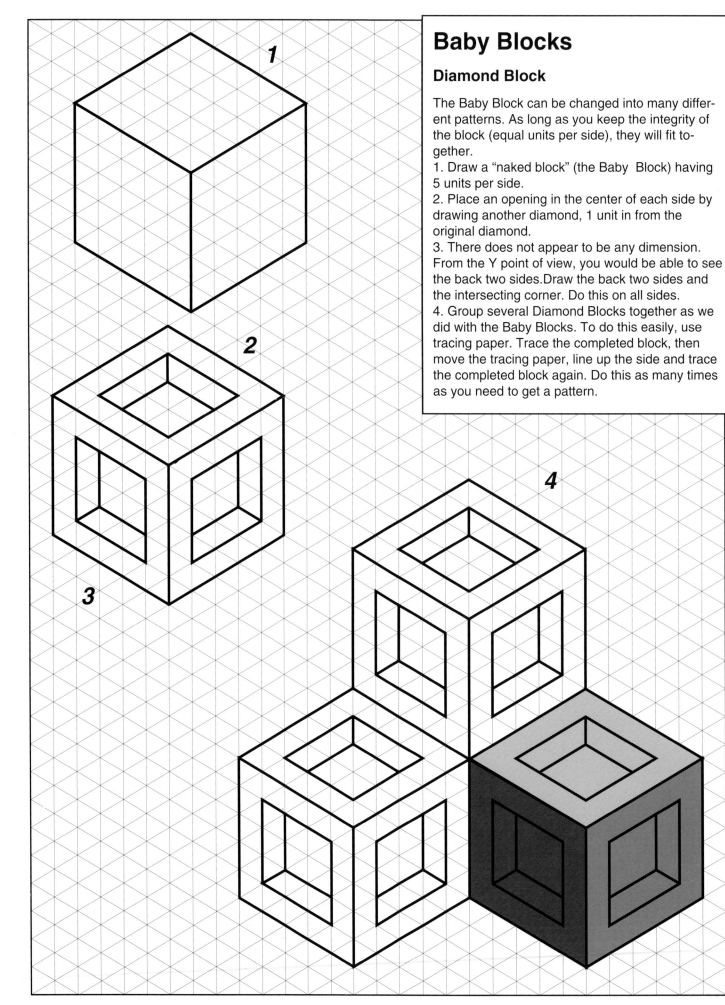

Baby Blocks

Diamond Block

The Baby Block can be changed into many different patterns. As long as you keep the integrity of the block (equal units per side), they will fit together.

1. Draw a "naked block" (the Baby Block) having 5 units per side.

2. Place an opening in the center of each side by drawing another diamond, 1 unit in from the original diamond.

3. There does not appear to be any dimension. From the Y point of view, you would be able to see the back two sides. Draw the back two sides and the intersecting corner. Do this on all sides.

4. Group several Diamond Blocks together as we did with the Baby Blocks. To do this easily, use tracing paper. Trace the completed block, then move the tracing paper, line up the side and trace the completed block again. Do this as many times as you need to get a pattern.

Baby Blocks

Rocks

The basic block can be changed by dividing it into several different pieces.

1. Draw a naked block consisting of 4 units per side.
2. Draw lines parallel to the inside Y of the block, 1 unit in.
3. Add a 2-unit diamond in the outside corner of each side. To give this dimension, the sides are needed.
4. Draw the sides of the smaller block by adding lines, toward the center, from the three corners.
5. Using tracing paper, trace the completed Rocks block. Move the tracing paper, line up the edges and group several blocks together.

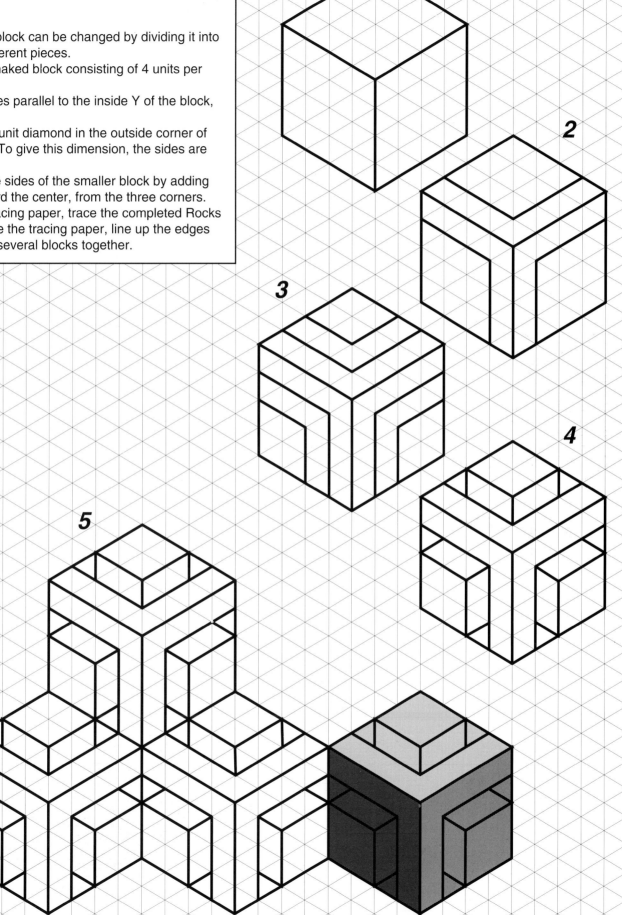

13

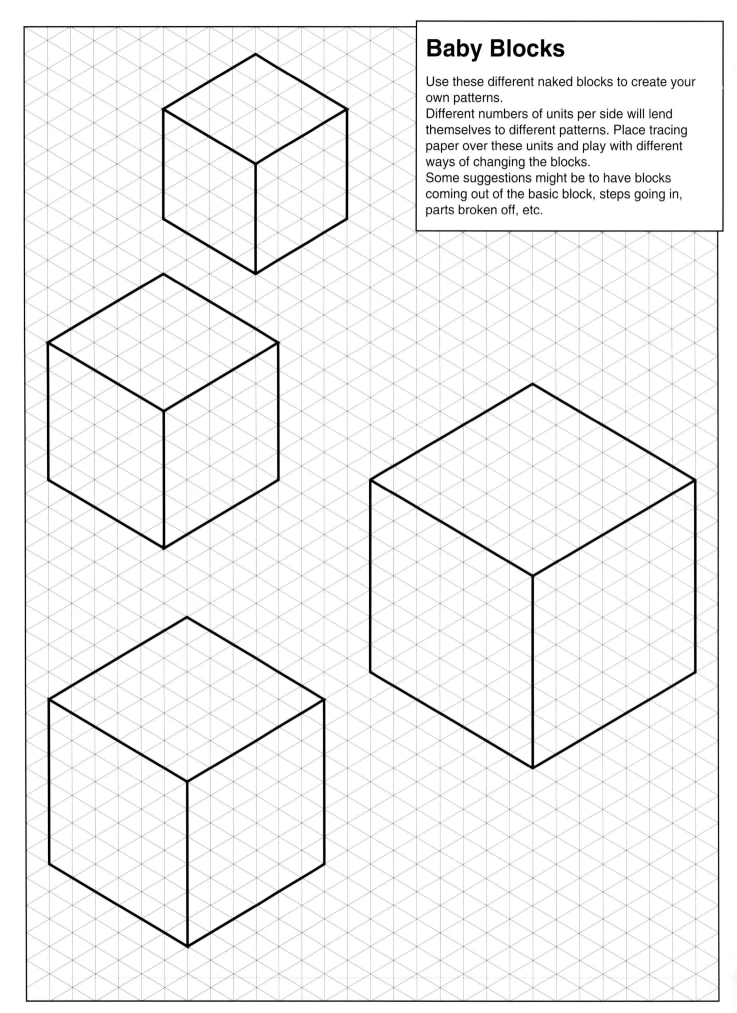

Baby Blocks

Use these different naked blocks to create your own patterns.

Different numbers of units per side will lend themselves to different patterns. Place tracing paper over these units and play with different ways of changing the blocks.

Some suggestions might be to have blocks coming out of the basic block, steps going in, parts broken off, etc.

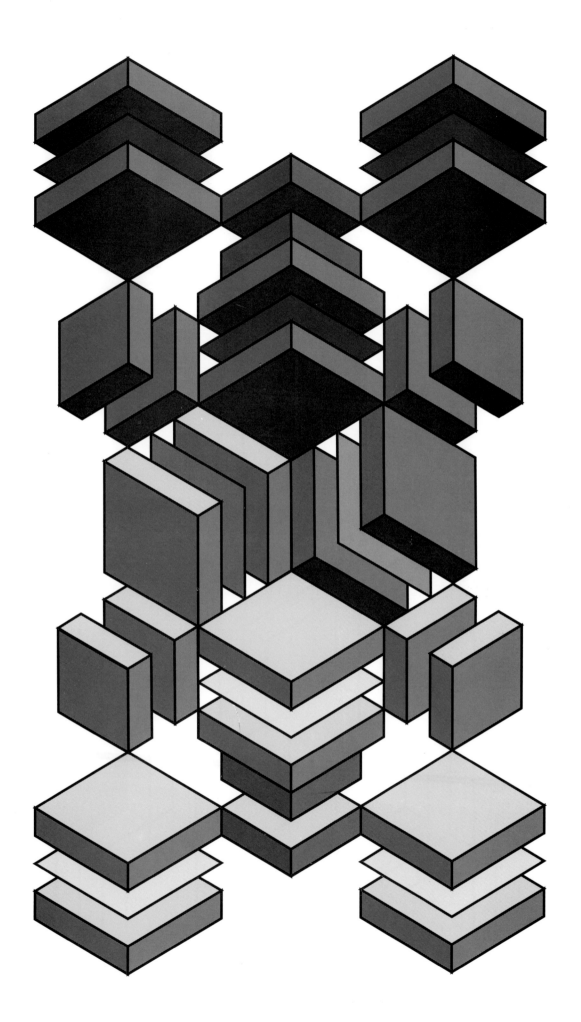

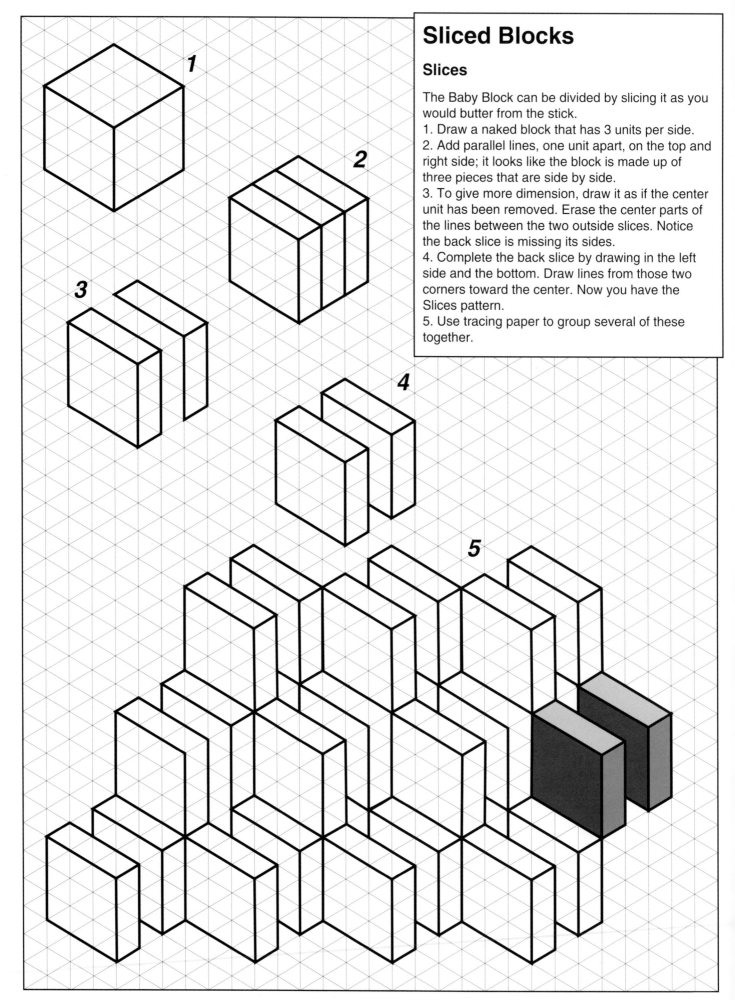

Sliced Blocks

Slices

The Baby Block can be divided by slicing it as you would butter from the stick.

1. Draw a naked block that has 3 units per side.

2. Add parallel lines, one unit apart, on the top and right side; it looks like the block is made up of three pieces that are side by side.

3. To give more dimension, draw it as if the center unit has been removed. Erase the center parts of the lines between the two outside slices. Notice the back slice is missing its sides.

4. Complete the back slice by drawing in the left side and the bottom. Draw lines from those two corners toward the center. Now you have the Slices pattern.

5. Use tracing paper to group several of these together.

Sliced Blocks

Sandwich

Multiple sliced divisions can be developed, depending on the number of units used per side. One possibility is to insert a paper-thin piece between two slices.

1. Draw a naked block that is 4 units per side.
2. Add three parallel lines, on the top and right sides.
3. Remove the center two slices by erasing the two parts of the lines to the left and right of the center line (on the top, center and bottom).
4. Now there are two thick pieces on either side of a paper-thin piece. Notice the back slice and the center paper-thin piece are missing sides. Complete these by extending lines from the two corners toward the center.
5. Use tracing paper to group several of these together.

Try some of your own sliced designs, using the different blocks on page 14.

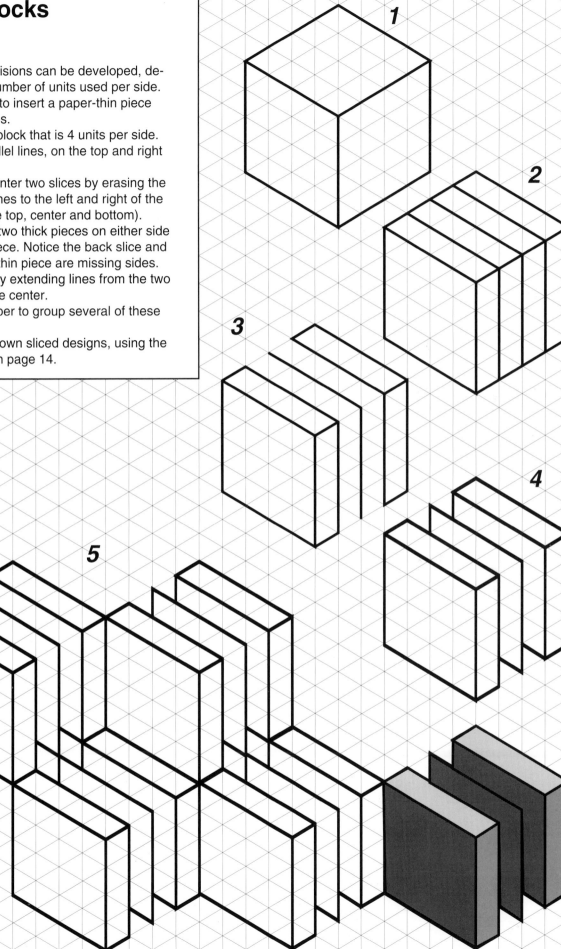

Interlocking Blocks

Cards

One side of the block is the isometric diamond and offers various possibilities for patterns that interlock.

1. Draw one 3-unit isometric diamond.
2. One way to create a pattern is to group them side by side.
3. A more interesting design is created by overlapping the diamonds. Draw a grouping of diamonds that overlap at the 120° angle by 1 unit.
4. This illusion of overlapping diamonds can also be achieved by overlapping two units.
5. On tracing paper, group several together into a row. Place several rows together. Place the first diamond of the next row so the top 60° corner sits between diamonds one and two from the previous row.

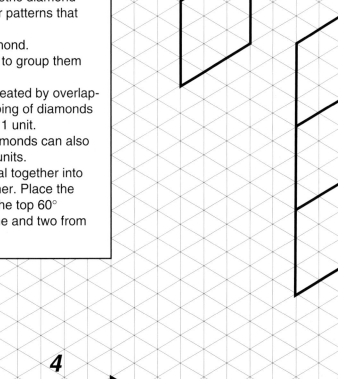

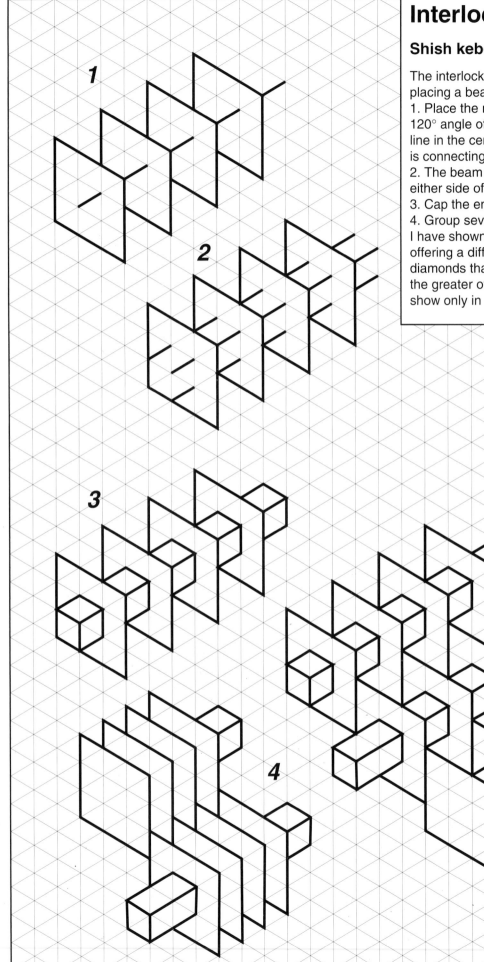

Interlocking Blocks

Shish kebob

The interlocking diamonds can be enhanced by placing a beam through the diamonds.

1. Place the ruler diagonally through the center 120° angle of all the diamonds and draw a 1-unit line in the center of each. It appears as if a thread is connecting the diamonds.

2. The beam will be one unit wide. Draw a line on either side of the center diagonal.

3. Cap the ends of the beam segments.

4. Group several rows together.

I have shown 3 ways to begin the beams, each offering a different look. Place a beam through the diamonds that overlap by two units. Because of the greater overlap, the beam is hidden and will show only in the front and the back.

Interlocking Blocks

Iso's

A different pattern emerges when width is added to the paper-thin piece.

1. Draw a 3-unit diamond. Give it a 1-unit thickness by adding lines from the three corners on the right.

2. Complete the diamond by adding lines for the side and top. (This is one part of the Slice pattern). All that is needed is the beam that will run through the slices. In Shish kebob, the beam was one unit wide by one unit long. In Iso's, the beam will still be one unit wide but it will need to be two units long to accommodate the added 1-unit thickness of the slice.

3. Draw the center of the beam from the bottom left corner of the diamond, 2 units in.

4. Draw the beam one unit wide.

5. Erase the part of the diamond that wouldn't show behind the beam.

6. Using tracing paper, group these to create an all-over interlocking pattern.

7. The pieces that end the beam will be complete diamonds.

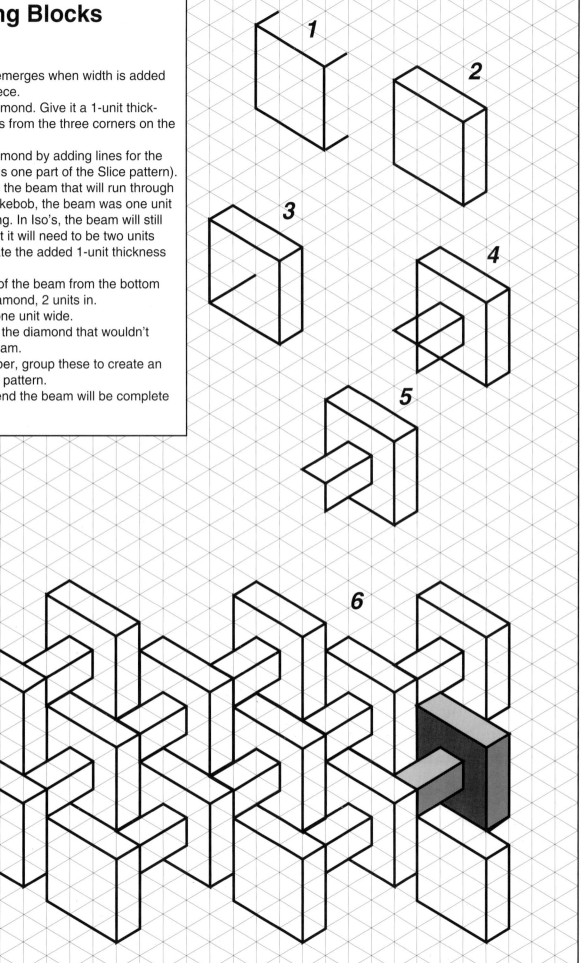

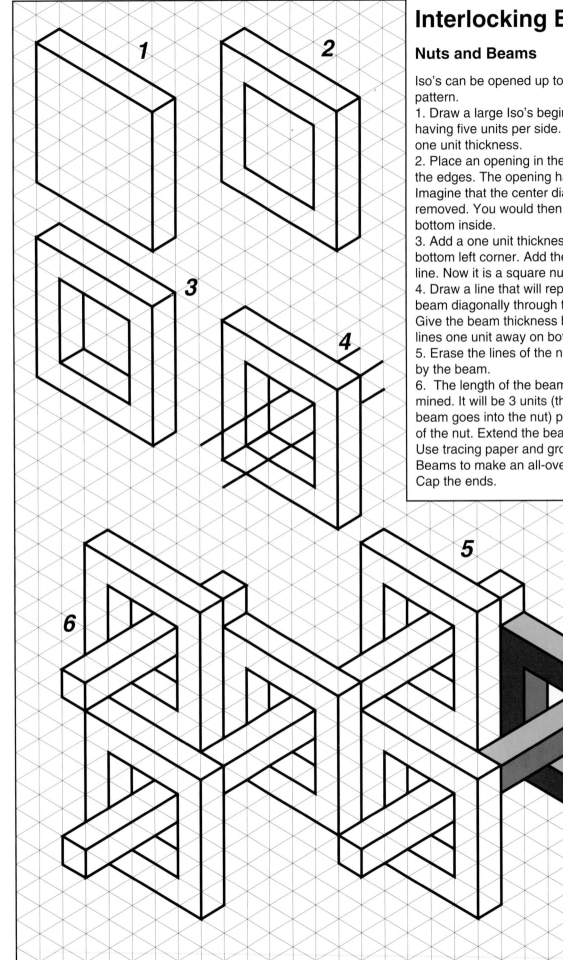

Interlocking Blocks

Nuts and Beams

Iso's can be opened up to achieve the Nut pattern.

1. Draw a large Iso's beginning with a diamond having five units per side. Give the diamond a one unit thickness.

2. Place an opening in the front, one unit in from the edges. The opening has no dimension. Imagine that the center diamond has been removed. You would then see the back and the bottom inside.

3. Add a one unit thickness from the inside bottom left corner. Add the back side and bottom line. Now it is a square nut.

4. Draw a line that will represent the center of the beam diagonally through the opening in the nut. Give the beam thickness by drawing two parallel lines one unit away on both sides.

5. Erase the lines of the nut that would be hidden by the beam.

6. The length of the beam needs to be determined. It will be 3 units (the number of units the beam goes into the nut) plus 1 unit for the width of the nut. Extend the beam 4 units.

Use tracing paper and group several Nuts and Beams to make an all-over interlocking pattern. Cap the ends.

Interlocking Blocks

Inner City

Another interlocking pattern is created by overlapping Baby Blocks.

1. Begin by drawing a naked block, 2 units per side.

2. Add three more blocks, each overlapping the first by one unit. Use a dotted line to indicate where the new blocks are behind the original. The resulting shape of the original block becomes the pattern for Inner City.

3. Using tracing paper, trace the new shape.

4. Move the tracing paper and group several together to create the all-over pattern.

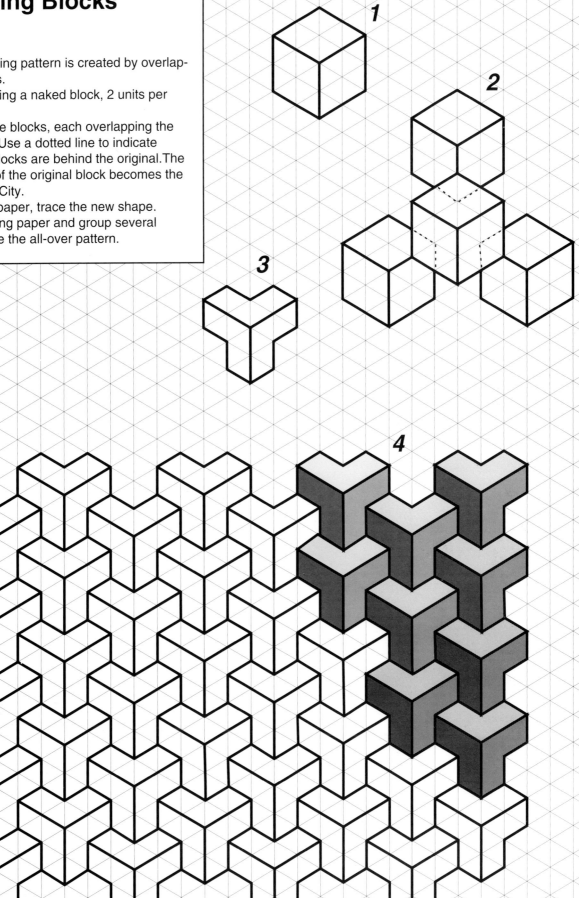

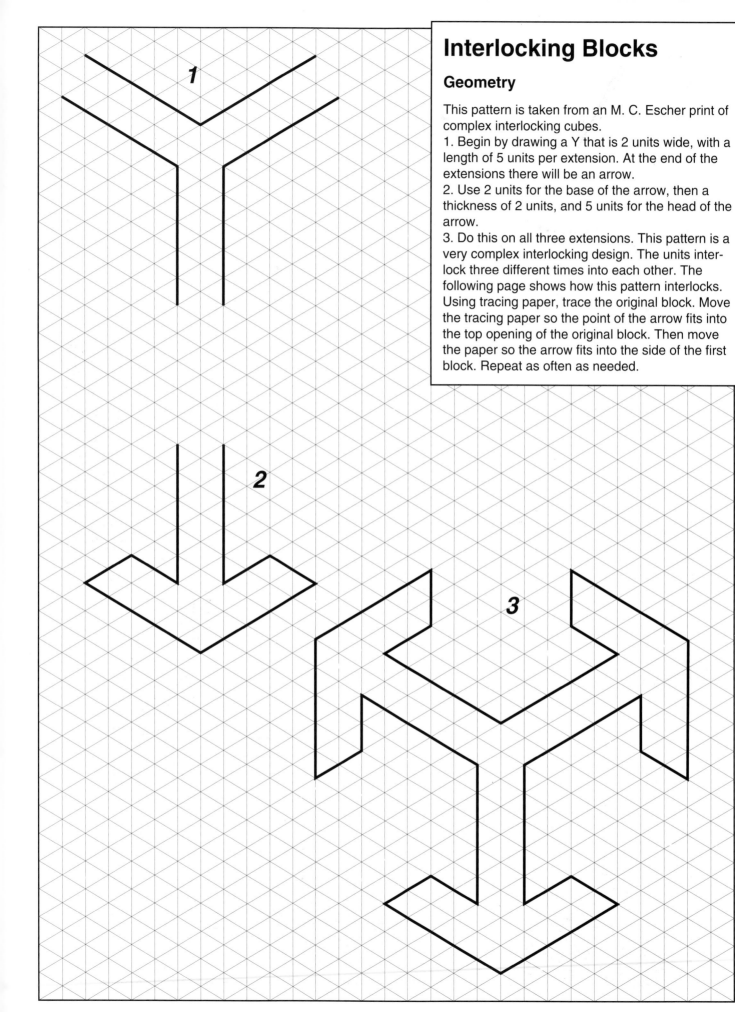

Interlocking Blocks

Geometry

This pattern is taken from an M. C. Escher print of complex interlocking cubes.

1. Begin by drawing a Y that is 2 units wide, with a length of 5 units per extension. At the end of the extensions there will be an arrow.

2. Use 2 units for the base of the arrow, then a thickness of 2 units, and 5 units for the head of the arrow.

3. Do this on all three extensions. This pattern is a very complex interlocking design. The units interlock three different times into each other. The following page shows how this pattern interlocks. Using tracing paper, trace the original block. Move the tracing paper so the point of the arrow fits into the top opening of the original block. Then move the paper so the arrow fits into the side of the first block. Repeat as often as needed.

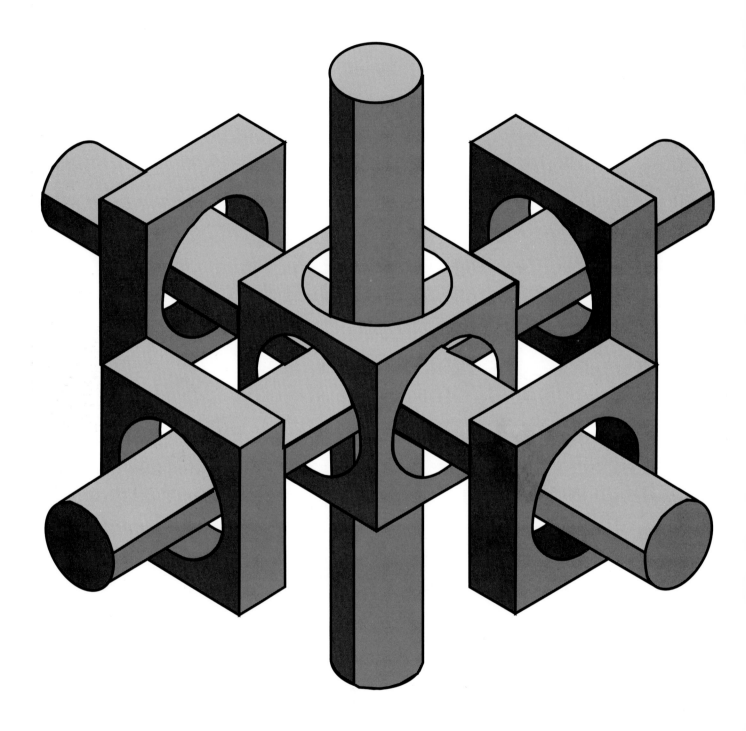

Isometric Circles

Holes

Circles can add more interest and movement to a design. There is a simple way to draw an isometric circle accurately within an isometric diamond.

1. Draw a diamond that has 8 units per side. Give it a 2-unit thickness.

2. Place the isometric ellipse template over the block, and find the ellipse that best fits the space; 1¾" has been used here. Line up the reference marks with the center of each side so the ellipse is evenly centered. Draw the ellipse.

3. Measure the thickness of the block with a ruler. It should be ½". The thickness of the hole should be the same. Measure ½" in from the center edge of the circle. Lay the same template opening, 1¾", over the block. Rest the top edge of the opening on the mark (center the verticle reference marks). Draw the part of the ellipse that you would see through the hole.

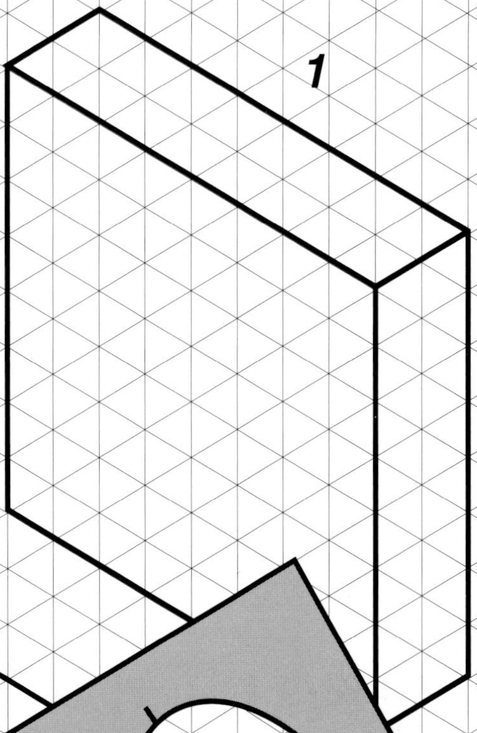

1

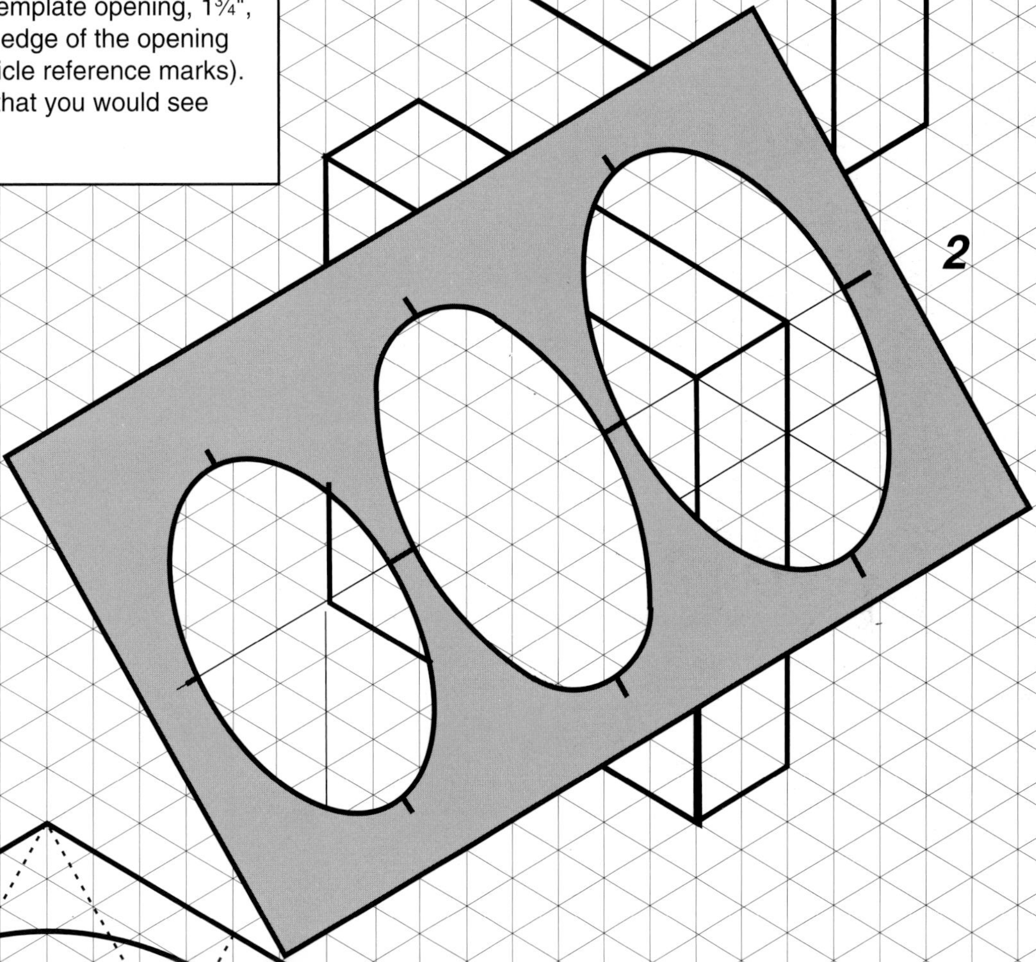

2

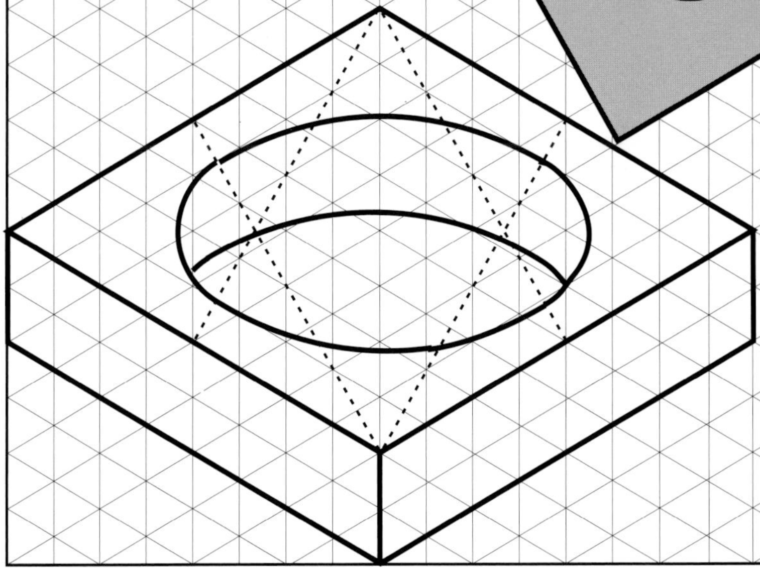

3

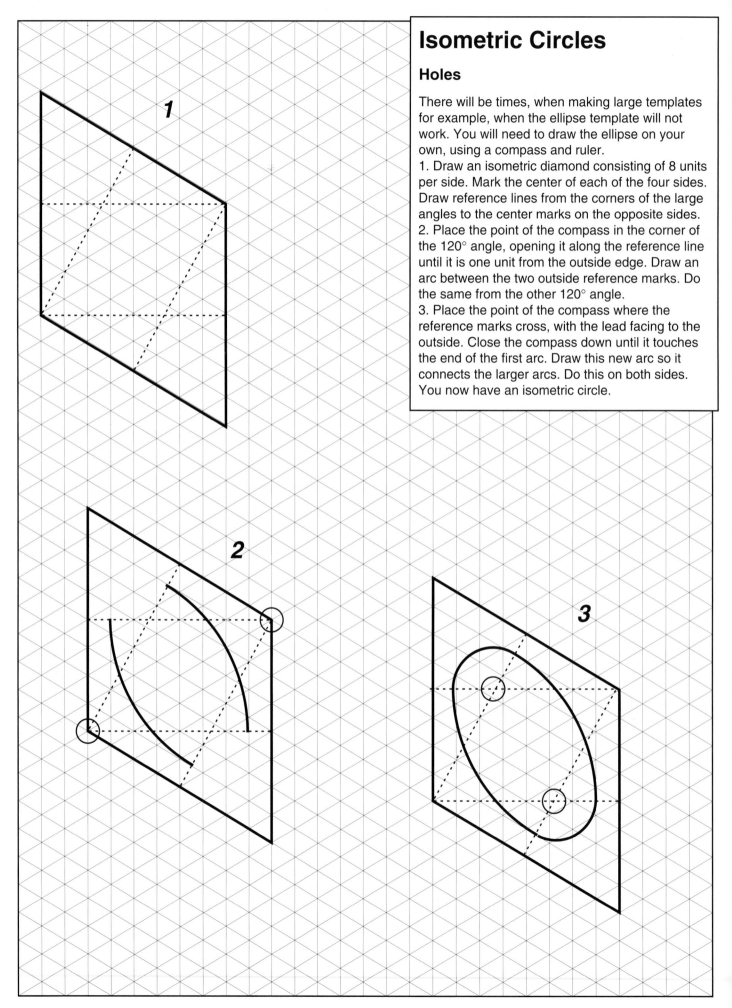

Isometric Circles

Holes

There will be times, when making large templates for example, when the ellipse template will not work. You will need to draw the ellipse on your own, using a compass and ruler.

1. Draw an isometric diamond consisting of 8 units per side. Mark the center of each of the four sides. Draw reference lines from the corners of the large angles to the center marks on the opposite sides.

2. Place the point of the compass in the corner of the 120° angle, opening it along the reference line until it is one unit from the outside edge. Draw an arc between the two outside reference marks. Do the same from the other 120° angle.

3. Place the point of the compass where the reference marks cross, with the lead facing to the outside. Close the compass down until it touches the end of the first arc. Draw this new arc so it connects the larger arcs. Do this on both sides. You now have an isometric circle.

Isometric Circles

Holes

1. Give the block from the previous page a 1-unit thickness. Add the bottom and side. Now it looks as if an isometric circle is drawn on the surface. Imagine that the circle has been lifted away; you would see the inside.

2. The thickness of the inside circle needs to be the same as the thickness of the block. Open your compass to the setting used to make the first two arcs of the hole (place the compass point on the 120° angle and open it to the large arc). The length of that center line is greater than the thickness of the block. Place the end of the ruler on the edge of the block. The width of this block should measure ½".

3. Measure ½" from the inside corner of the isometric block. That is where to place the point of the compass.

Draw the bottom of the circle. *This arc actually needs to come in a little more sharply at the ends. Because the bend is so slight I find it easier to do it freehand. Just bring the arc in slightly to echo the outside curve.*

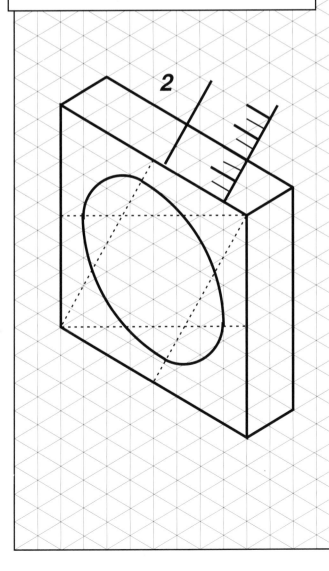
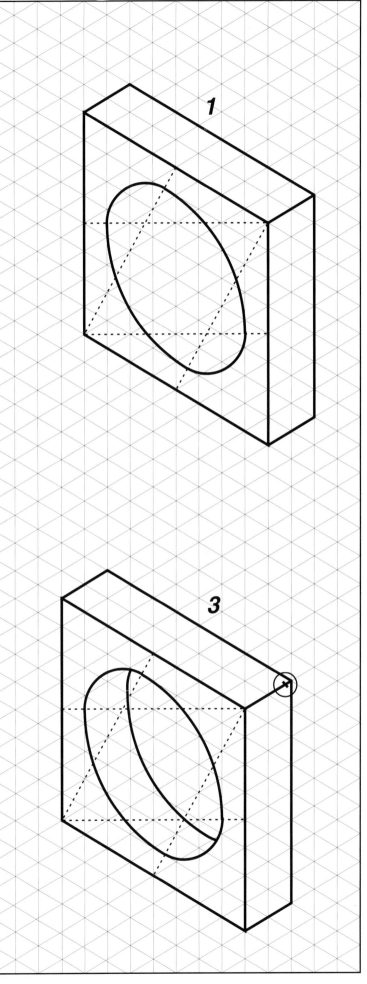

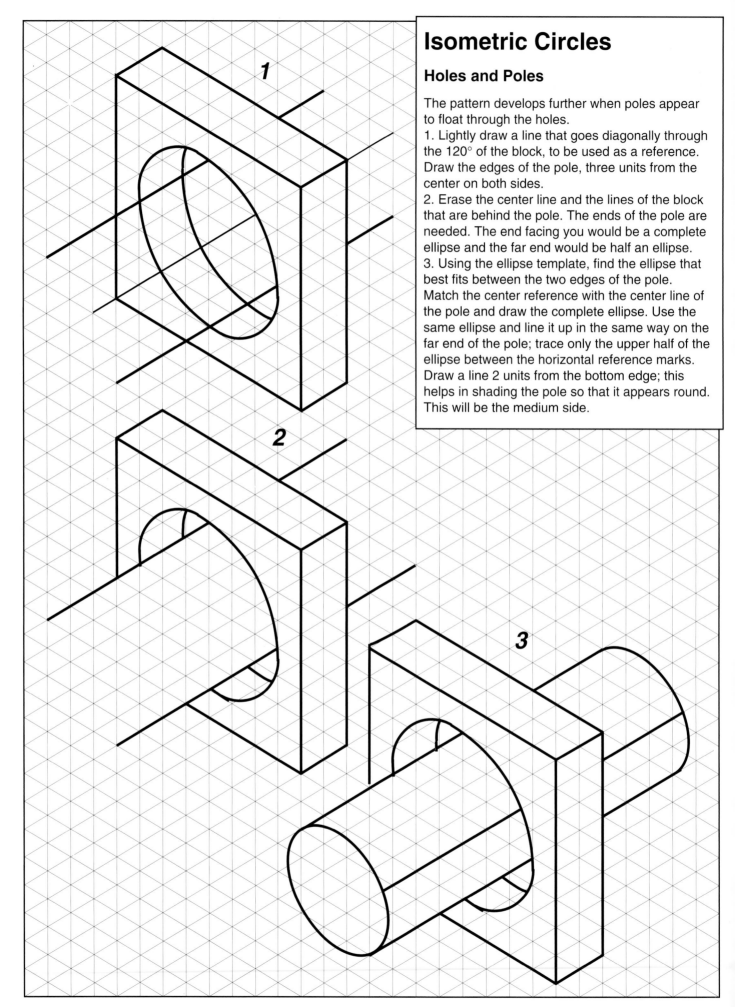

Isometric Circles

Holes and Poles

The pattern develops further when poles appear to float through the holes.

1. Lightly draw a line that goes diagonally through the 120° of the block, to be used as a reference. Draw the edges of the pole, three units from the center on both sides.

2. Erase the center line and the lines of the block that are behind the pole. The ends of the pole are needed. The end facing you would be a complete ellipse and the far end would be half an ellipse.

3. Using the ellipse template, find the ellipse that best fits between the two edges of the pole. Match the center reference with the center line of the pole and draw the complete ellipse. Use the same ellipse and line it up in the same way on the far end of the pole; trace only the upper half of the ellipse between the horizontal reference marks. Draw a line 2 units from the bottom edge; this helps in shading the pole so that it appears round. This will be the medium side.

Isometric Circles

Holes and Poles

Using tracing paper, group several Holes and Poles together. Remember to figure the length of the poles by counting the number of units needed for inside of the block (4) plus the number of units for the width of the block (2). These Holes and Poles can be drawn on the diagonal or can be turned, as I have done, so that the poles are vertical.

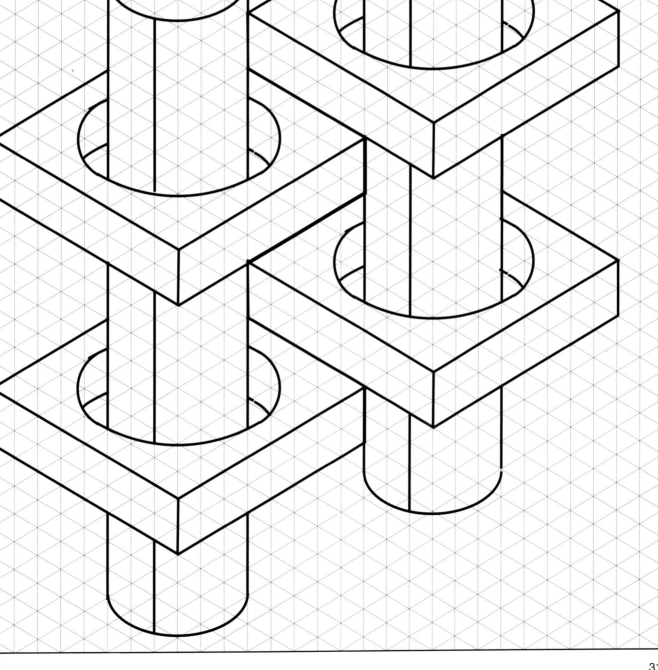

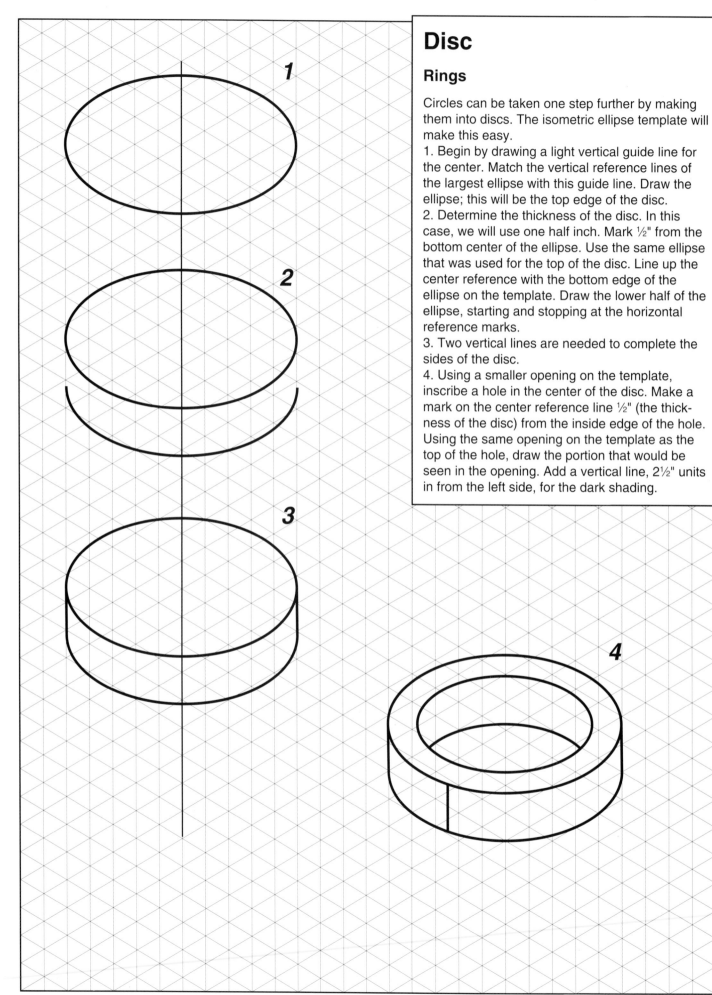

Disc

Rings

Circles can be taken one step further by making them into discs. The isometric ellipse template will make this easy.

1. Begin by drawing a light vertical guide line for the center. Match the vertical reference lines of the largest ellipse with this guide line. Draw the ellipse; this will be the top edge of the disc.

2. Determine the thickness of the disc. In this case, we will use one half inch. Mark ½" from the bottom center of the ellipse. Use the same ellipse that was used for the top of the disc. Line up the center reference with the bottom edge of the ellipse on the template. Draw the lower half of the ellipse, starting and stopping at the horizontal reference marks.

3. Two vertical lines are needed to complete the sides of the disc.

4. Using a smaller opening on the template, inscribe a hole in the center of the disc. Make a mark on the center reference line ½" (the thickness of the disc) from the inside edge of the hole. Using the same opening on the template as the top of the hole, draw the portion that would be seen in the opening. Add a vertical line, 2½" units in from the left side, for the dark shading.

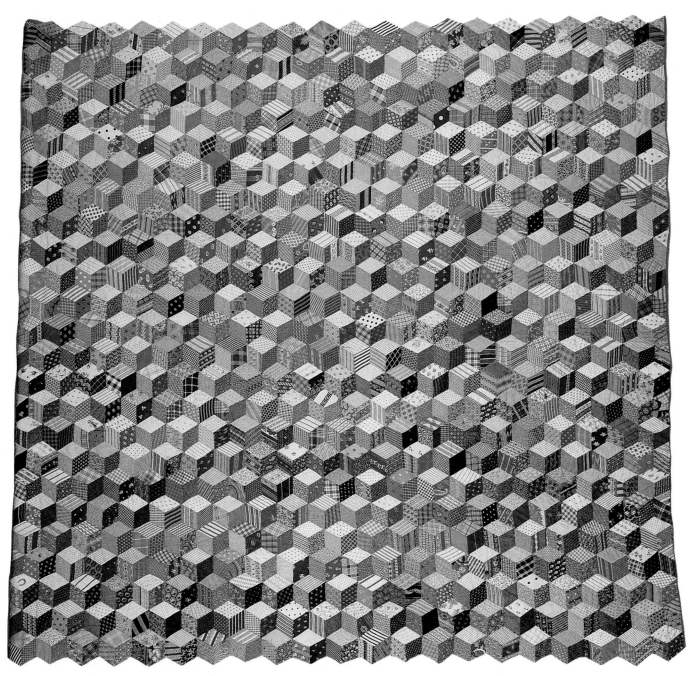

PLATE 1. **Tumbling Blocks** (c. 1875) courtesy of Charlotte Ekback.
83" x 80". Hand pieced, hand quilted recently by Birds in the Air quilting group of Moorpark, CA.
This is a wonderful example of one of the first quilting patterns (Baby Blocks) based on isometrics. It is an excellent example of light, medium, and dark coloration in a scrap quilt.

PLATE 2. **Inner City** by Jinny Beyer, Great Falls, VA.
80" x 92". Hand pieced, hand quilted.
I began this quilt in January 1978 and completed it in July 1980. I made it for my son Darren. I enjoy working with the isometric patterns. One may arrive at an idea and think it an original, then several weeks later, as in my case, see a similar design in several different sources. **Inner City** is an old historic Islamic pattern found in tile work and ornaments of past centuries.

PLATE 3. **Labyrinth** by Katie, from the collection of Bob Masopust, Sr.
90" x 85". Hand and machine pieced, hand quilted.
This layered design consists of over 200 Iso's, in black, for the background. The second layer is Baby Blocks and Slices with ellipses; the foreground is Beams and Blocks with ellipses. The original drawing had no ellipses, but I enjoy working with the curved line. After being shown how to draft an ellipse accurately, I added many of them for a more interesting design.

PLATE 4. **Wedding Quilt** by Katie.
51" x 63". Hand and machine pieced, hand quilted.
Wedding Quilt combines Holes and Poles and stacked isometric boxes with different things happening in each one. There are several appliquéd rings and various other symbols, representing parts of our lives, scattered throughout. It hung as a backdrop at our outdoor wedding ceremony.

PLATE 5. **Bearding Pedestrian** by Katie, courtesy of Randi and Mike Perkins.
56" x 66". Machine pieced, hand quilted.
In order to reach a deadline, this quilt was designed and pieced in one week. To reach this goal, I designed it with large and simplified Iso's for the background and large Slices in the foreground. Upon completion, I felt the top of the quilt was too empty, so I added paper-thin diamonds that appear to float and twist away. At first glance the drawing seemed simple or pedestrian, and I used a different batting than usual, one which kept bearding, hence the strange title.

PLATE 6. **Dimensional Portal** by Katie.
83" x 83". Hand and machine pieced, hand quilted.
My first thought was to create something that the viewer would want to get into and climb about on (like we did as kids on the bars at the park). I used three layers of beams and poles to create this illusion. I added some little silver beads to the black background to give a greater illusion of depth. My stepson, Bob III, named this one; he said it was like looking through a hole into another dimension.

PLATE 7. **Glacier** by Katie.
113" x 79". Hand and machine pieced, hand quilted.
I went on a wonderful Alaskan cruise in the summer of 1990. The highlight of the cruise was the glacier at the end of the Tracy Arm. We heard and saw a chunk break off! A majestic bald eagle flew by, and the sun came out for the first time all day. I came home, filled my studio with photos of the glacier, and created this quilt, using an impressionistic design. The photo inset shows a portion of the glacier. There are actually four more photos which, when put into place, show the complete glacier. The resulting quilt would be wider than I care to imagine, so just the ends were put together to produce a more workable design.

PLATE 8. **My Secret Garden** by Katie.
56" x 70". Hand and machine pieced, hand quilted.
I found a picture of a garden in a flower book. It was a very inviting garden that
I wanted for my own. Since I don't have a green thumb, I realized the only way
to have it would be to quilt it. The different isometric blocks represent different
plants and paths. I quilted it in leaves and flowers. I then felt that the lines were
too hard and the quilting obscure. To soften the quilt, I took a paint brush and
fabric paint and proceeded to paint the negative space behind the quilted
leaves and flowers.

PLATE 9. **Mardi Gras** by Katie, courtesy of Randi and Mike Perkins.
33" x 22". Machine pieced, hand quilted.
Geometrics is a great pattern to use to interlock and blend colors. The Hoffman fabric in the background was the inspiration for the title.

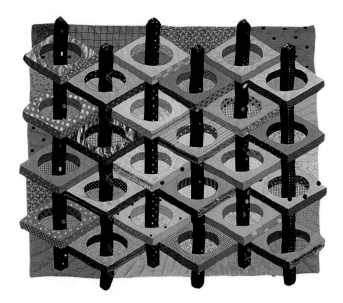

PLATE 10. **Holes and Poles** by Katie, courtesy of Diane Coombs.
20" x 18". Hand and machine pieced, hand quilted.
I made **Holes and Poles** in order to perfect my reverse appliqué of the ellipses. I alternated cool and warm colors because I enjoy all the colors in the color wheel.

PLATE 11. **Iso's 1** by Katie, courtesy of Judi Wagner, photo by Tony van Hasselt.
23" x 23". Hand pieced, hand quilted.
This Iso's quilt was a study of shades of gray, moving from light in the upper left corner to dark in the lower right corner, with the dark side being all blacks.

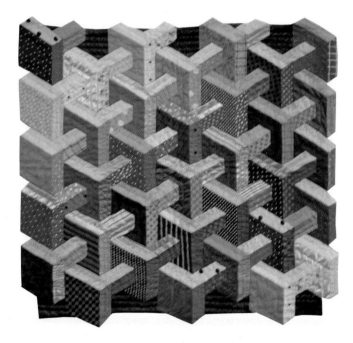

PLATE 12. **Iso's 2** by Katie, courtesy of the Teeboons, photo by Katie.
23" x 23". Machine pieced, hand quilted.
After exploring the shading of gray, the second step was to create a color wheel within the Iso's block. Each row was light, medium, and dark within its own color, repeating the yellow and green to keep the motion going.

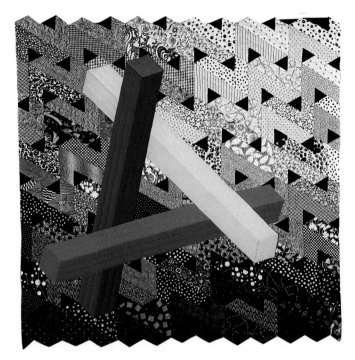

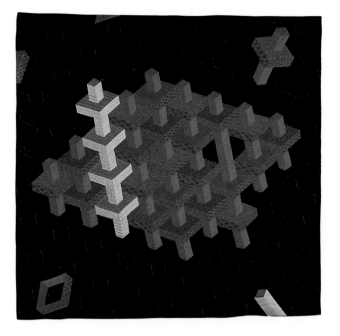

PLATE 13. **N-Iso** by Nancy Morgan, Merritt Island, FL.
41" x 40". Machine pieced, machine quilted.
I have always wanted to do a black and white quilt with bright colors as accents. The background is a result of tessellating the letter N. I chose to do the isometric foreground in bright, primary colors so it would float above the background.

PLATE 14. **Gridlock** by Wendy Hill, Nevada City, CA.
41" x 40". Machine pieced, hand and machine quilted.
"What if the units are physically on the same plane but part of the structure appears closer?" I kept having images of a gridlock in space, units being pulled by gravity. I see the units coming together, but most viewers think the structure appears to be fragmenting and breaking apart. It's all an illusion.

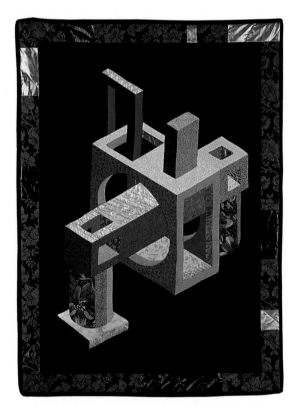

PLATE 15. **Hubble, Hubble...What Do You See?**
by Cindy Blackberg, Kissimmee, FL.
55" x 63". Hand and machine pieced, hand quilted.
The idea for the quilt came from the media hype over the Hubble Telescope, which was supposed to send back pictures that showed our origins. This is a tongue-in-cheek look at what the Hubble might have seen if the mirror had not broken.

PLATE 16. **Friendly Support** by Charlane McCurdy, Fairbanks, AK.
28" x 38". Machine pieced, hand and machine quilted.
I wanted to create an isometric environment that had beams and poles, with openings and places to hide. I call it **Friendly Support**, in honor of my many quilting friends who helped me through a very difficult time.

PLATE 17. **Interweave** by Julie Sowards, Fairbanks, AK. *22" x 17". Machine pieced, hand quilted.*
I have been quilting for fifteen years, and Katie's classes gave me lots of information of which I was unaware. I am sure that I will be using these isometric techniques and sets in innumerable ways.

PLATE 18. **Corks a' Poppin'** by Rebecca Steinmetz, St. Louis, MO.
37" x 37". Hand and machine pieced, hand and machine quilted.
I was inspired by designs in the book *Triads and Optical Illusions*. I had the knowledge to complete my idea after the isometric class with Katie. I have set my isometric blocks within the hexagon shape.

PLATE 19. **Rain Forest Creation** by Phoebe Bartleet, Romsey, Hants, England; photo courtesy of Phoebe.
40" x 30". Machine pieced, hand quilted.
I wanted to give the impression of trees and tree trunks. The floating blocks at the top of the design indicate tree tops. I experimented with many fabrics for the border and background but felt that the jade brought the whole design together.

PLATE 20. **Pillars of Society** by Virda Wilcox Lawrence, Gig Harbor, WA.

75" x 99". Hand pieced, hand quilted.

There are 1,958 different textiles in this charm quilt. There are fabrics from the 1800s through, and including, today's neons. Every holiday is represented. The fabrics were collected from quilters all over the world. This project was a true color study for me. Based on the light, medium, dark premise, I put colors together in the five-piece Iso's.

There are many recognizable fun pieces in this quilt: Mickey Mouse, Little Bo Peep, Campbell Soup Kid, ducks, birds, etc. This quilt is a babysitter for my grandchildren. They will spread it out and we play a game: "Who can find a chicken?" The first one who finds the chicken gets a hug from grandma; then it's who can find a bear, flower, bird, etc.

PLATE 21. **Make New Friends, But Keep the Old** by Kathy Marx, Nolensville, TN.

47" x 75". Machine and hand pieced, hand quilted.

This is a tribute to all of my supportive friends from throughout the U.S. and Canada. This is my first original-design quilt. I am a traditionalist. The isometric blocks represent my new friends, and traditional patchwork represents my old friends.

PLATE 22. **Quilsars: A Celestial Phenomenon**
by Suzann Semonovick, Palm Coast, FL.
33" x 39". Hand and machine pieced, hand quilted.
Isometric designs have always interested me. It is fun and exciting to watch as my design takes on depth and dimension with every piece of fabric I add. **Quilsars** was made as a challenge piece. It uses Jeffery Gutcheon's diamond patchwork method for the main design and isometric designs from Katie's class.

PLATE 23. **Things that Go Bump in the Night**
by Carole Steiner, Santa Maria, CA.
41" x 45". Hand and machine pieced, hand quilted.
With isometrics, I can create my own designs with limitless possibilities. I am basically what most people would call a traditional quilter, but I have a great sense of adventure, and isometrics gave me the chance to express my own creativity. Katie has that special way of tapping into our creativity in order to design a quilt that is truly our own.

PLATE 24. **Tumbling Kleenex Boxes** by Carol Rothrock, Nordland, WA.
29" x 23". Machine pieced, hand quilted.
The most useful technique that I learned from this project was setting the colored blocks into the solid black background. I selected bright rainbow colors to go against the black. A wide variety of hand dyed, marbled, silk screened, and lamé fabrics were used.

PLATE 25. **Iso's** by Betsy Lopresto, Morro Bay, CA.
48" x 43". Machine and hand pieced, machine quilted.
When I heard of the isometric perspective class, I felt it was way beyond me, but I was curious. I loved every minute of it, including the drafting! I am so proud of my Iso's quilt that it hangs on my living room wall!

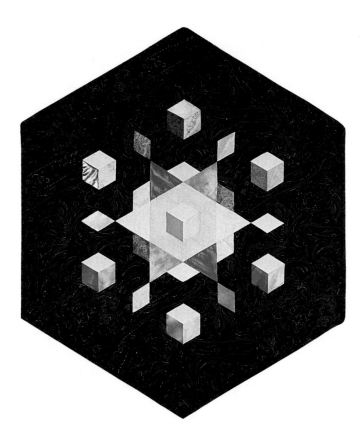

PLATE 26. **Diamonds Make Stars in My Ice Cube**
by Gail Flodin, Fairbanks, AK, photo by James Barker.
33" x 39". Machine pieced, hand quilted.
I knew I had succeeded with the transparency when I was asked,
"Was it hard to quilt through all the layers where they overlapped?"
I made each small cube reflect light from within.

PLATE 27. **An Isometric Class** by Jan Brashears, Atlanta, GA.
45" x 40". Hand and machine pieced, machine quilted.
This homework assignment piece was from the initial classwork
and lots of fun. The piecework was done by hand as I traveled
around. The machine quilting was an experiment. The piece
never fails to get attention; most people comment, "It looks so
complicated."

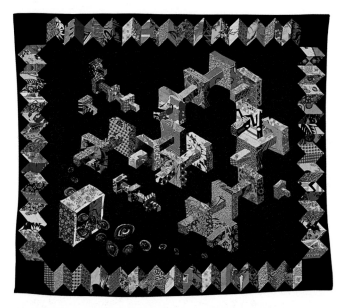

PLATE 28. **Isometric Eyesore** by Julie Rowe Johnston,
Goleta, CA.
54" x 44". Machine and hand pieced, hand quilted.
This quilt is called **Isometric Eyesore** because it is composed
of a variety of ugly fabrics. I belong to a computer group on
GEnie. We had a fabric swap, and I received sixty 10" squares
of the most horrible looking fabric! In the middle of the night the
work eyesore appeared, and then it automatically hooked up
with isometrics. One of the fabrics was all eyeballs....I was one
of the few that used this fabric in the challenge.

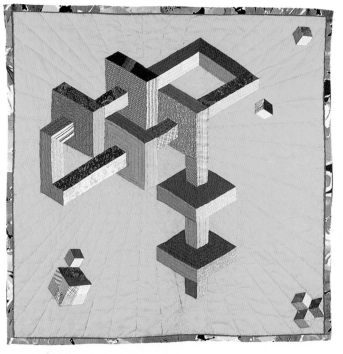

PLATE 29. **Isometrick** by Janice Lee Baehr, Snohomish, WA.
34" x 36". Machine pieced, hand quilted.
These techniques opened my eyes to the fact that anything
that can be represented with lines on paper can be reproduced
in fabric on a quilt. I particularly wanted to incorporate an optical
illusion into the shape that was afloat in space, and I accom-
plished that illusion with the placement of the light, medium,
and dark surfaces. I like the fun and surprises of scrappy quilts,
so I chose to use many fabrics to create my **Isometrick**.

46

PLATE 30. **My Challenge** by Agnes Ronat, Mt. Vernon, IL.
39" x 43". Machine pieced, hand quilted.
I chose the color wheel for my design. Since I can't draw or
sketch, isometric graph paper makes it a joy to complete a
pattern like this. I was completely absorbed in my project until
I was finished.

PLATE 31. **Lit from Within** by Judi Wagner,
E. Boothbay, ME.
21" x 33". Hand pieced, machine quilted.
This isometric exercise taught me to construct. I call it
Lit from Within because the lamé makes it glow.
Going through the steps to complete this piece gave
me confidence to try some other ideas of my own.

PLATE 32. **Moonlit Garden** by Jan Brashears, Atlanta, GA.
54" x 58". Machine pieced, hand quilted.
Moonlit Garden arrived as an impressionistic version of a garden of flowers and trees, lit only by the moon. The challenge was
to use the shading and idea in an isometric form. The hand quilting is free style. Isometric piecing and design gives me a new
view of dimension that challenges and excites my imagination.

PLATE 33. **Iso's** by Sandra Torguson,
Sacramento, CA.
16" x 16". Machine pieced, machine quilted.
This cheerful "throw around" (and/or utility)
pillow was a great way to use scraps, practice
turning corners, and learn about contrast of
light, medium, and dark fabrics.

PLATE 34. **Nuts and Bolts** by Margarite Wilson, Santa Fe, NM.
21" x 25". Machine pieced.
This was a fascinating project. While working on my piece, I was inspired to try other color variations. It is the combination of the geometric shape and the color that is so intriguing.

PLATE 35. **Nuts and Bolts** by Irene Strege, Albuquerque, NM.
21" x 25". Hand pieced.
Nuts and Bolts was an exciting and challenging wall hanging to make. Hand dyed cotton was used for the background. The five different colors and their range of values helped to create a visual illusion.

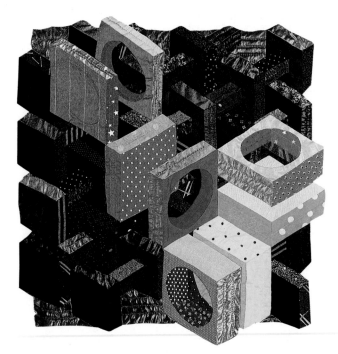

PLATE 36. **His** by Katie.
21" x 21". Hand and machine pieced, hand quilted.
This small sampler of isometric blocks was used to "test the waters" prior to piecing the larger version, **Labyrinth**. It was a gift to my husband for teaching me how to draft the isometric ellipse. The pattern Nuts and Bolts was conceived from this quilt; look closely and you will notice that there are a few differences. Please feel free to change and add to the pattern at the back of the book to make it your own.

Isometric Circles

Beams and Blocks

Isometric ellipses can be put on any isometric surface. The pattern Beams and Blocks is created by placing ellipses on all three surfaces of the naked block. Once the block has been opened up in this manner, it seems only natural to have something passing through the surfaces; here, a beam has been inserted.

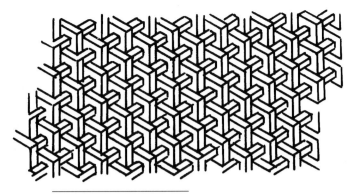

Background of Iso's

Layering

Labyrinth

Layering is one way of creating a dimensional design. In this section, I will show how I arrived at some of my quilts using this method. The best way to begin your own design is to play with the different isometric patterns: use tracing paper to draw the different layers. Then stack the layers to see how they interact with each other.

Labyrinth consists of three layers. The back layer is Iso's. The front layer is a combination of blocks and ellipses with beams passing through. The middle layer is Baby Blocks and Slices with ellipses (the ellipses were added at the template stage).

It is important to think about scale. You will notice that the background is made of smaller units. The further something is from you, the smaller it appears. In the next layer, the units are larger, with the front layer consisting of the largest pieces. This gives the feeling that you are looking through something that is close while viewing things in the distance.

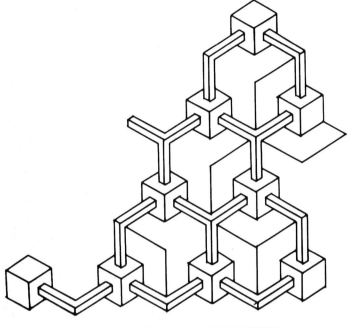

Front layer, Beams and Blocks

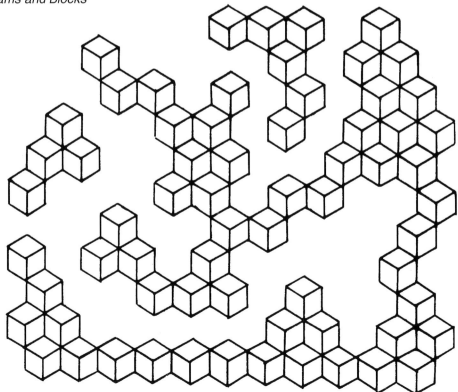

Middle layer, random Baby Blocks

Labyrinth—*a combination of the three layers*

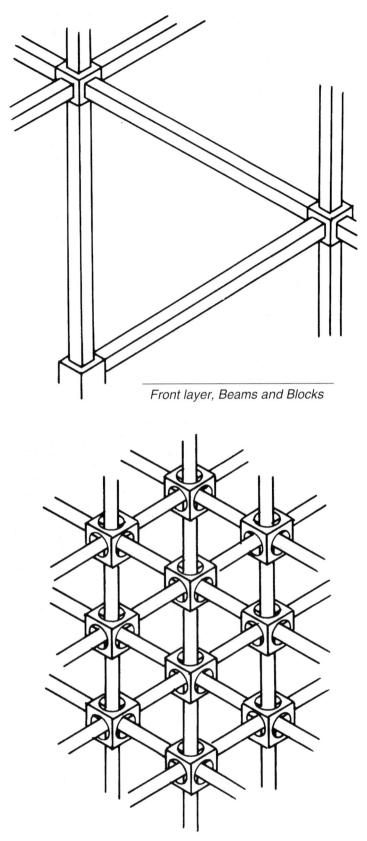

Front layer, Beams and Blocks

Layering

Dimensional Portal

I first visualized this quilt as several open layers that you could climb through. I felt that the layers had to be very open, so I made the beams between the blocks long and thin. This left room in the negative space to add more layers. I started by drawing the front layer on tracing paper. I worked on 22" tracing paper, taping four pieces of graph paper together to get the desired size.

The next layer is blocks with ellipses. There are poles that pass through the holes in the blocks. The length of the poles is shorter in this layer to create more interest. The final layer is a repeat of the first layer but much smaller, to give the feeling of distance.

These three layers were stacked in order; at first glance, I realized that the center layer had to be skewed a bit so all of the vertical lines weren't going in the same direction. A fourth tracing paper was placed on top and I copied what I had thought was the final drawing (top drawing on the next page).

Middle layer, blocks with ellipses and poles

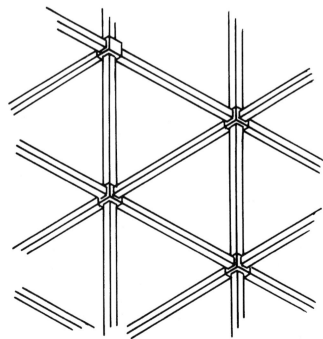

Back layer, a smaller version of the front layer

Layering

Dimensional Portal

It is very important to take time when developing a new design. At first, I thought that this was an OK design. When I pinned it to the wall and looked at it for some time, I realized there were some things I didn't like. First, the beams and blocks in the front layer are cut off at no reasonable point by the outside edge. The other thing I didn't like was the center layer. There seemed to be too many blocks, leaving no place to rest my eyes.

Using another piece of tracing paper, I traced the design, changing the outside edge to a circle, thus allowing the blocks and beams to overlap the edge. This seemed more inviting. I also eliminated a few of the blocks in the center layer, giving it more variety. Again I pinned it to the wall and studied it. There were still areas that didn't feel right. Even though some of the blocks had been removed, the center layer was still too busy. Also, there was not enough difference between the width of the beams in the back layer and the poles in the center.

I then placed a piece of tracing paper over the design and changed these details. Some of the poles were chopped off so they didn't extend over the whole quilt. The width of the center poles was increased and lines were added to create roundness.

As you can see, there are many steps leading to the final drawing.

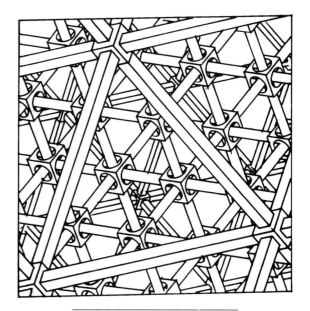

The three layers together

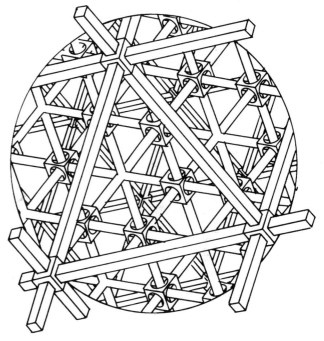

The three layers within a circle with several blocks in the middle layer removed

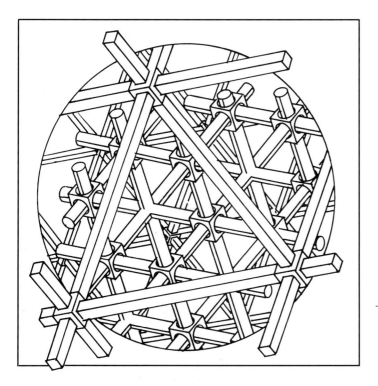

The final drawing

Drawing for wall hanging

Enlarging

Proportional Scale

Enlarging a completed design is easy if you have the correct tools. The first step is to have a design with which you are happy. How large the quilt will be is the next decision. Once you have decided that, you need to determine the proportion between the drawing and the quilt. The proportional scale is an invaluable tool. The most important thing to remember is that the drawing relates to the little wheel and the quilt relates to the big wheel. For example, our drawing is 3" wide. That number relates to the little wheel. The width of the quilt will be fifty inches. Find 50" on the big wheel and line up 3" with 50". The scale is now set for this project; do not move the wheels again. Tape them in place. If a measurement on the drawing is 2½", find that measurement on the little wheel. Look to the big wheel and it will show that the measurement will be 41¾" on the enlargement. If a measurement on the drawing is below 1", find 1" on the little wheel and look to the left at the fractions shown in a different color. This shows that the enlargement for ¾" is 16¾".

Proportional scale set for enlarging. Drawing is 3" wide (small wheel); quilt will be 50" wide (big wheel).

Enlarging

Matt Board

Tape lightweight matt board together until it is large enough to accommodate the size of the quilt. The example will be enlarged to 50" x 62" ($4\frac{7}{8}$" is the height of the drawing; find that measurement on the little wheel. The big wheel shows the width will be 62".).

Tape all of the edges together on the shiny side. Turn the whole thing over so the dull side is up (this side accepts pencil more readily and also erases more easily). Now you are ready to transfer the drawing. Locate a starting point. In this case, I would start with the bottom of the center line. Measure the distance from the bottom edge of the drawing. Find the enlargement on the proportional scale. Locate the center of the matt board and measure up for the starting point. Next measure the length of the center line; find the enlarged length on the scale and draw the line on the matt board. Use a protractor to copy the angles accurately. (See page 57 for more on angles and protractors.) Continue transferring all of the lines, one at a time. Relax, take it slowly and remember to enjoy yourself. When you are finished you will need to add reference marks at any point where a seam meets another seam (see page 58 for more on the importance of these marks).

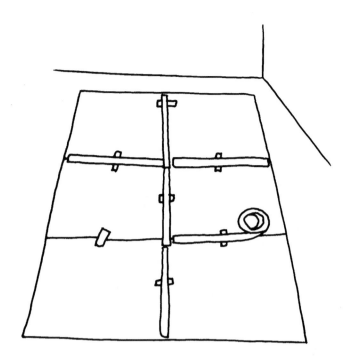

Matt board taped together for making templates

A protractor and proportional scale are used to enlarge the drawing onto the matt board.

Wall hanging of Rocks and Blocks

Enlarging

Graph Paper

If your pattern is a repeat of a single unit, templates need to be made for each piece of the block. Measure the width of the complete design; find that measurement on the little wheel of the proportional scale. Determine the width of the quilt and find that measure on the big wheel. Line these two figures up. Measure the side of the block. Find that measurement on the little wheel. Look to the big wheel and that will indicate how big the sides of the block will be. For example, if it shows the enlarged size will be 3½". Find how many units on the graph paper equal 3½" (12 units plus a bit). Round down to 12 units per side. Using the isometric graph paper, draft the block having 12 units per side. If the three sides are the same, as in this case, only one side of the block needs to be drawn. Draw the block onto the graph paper. Lay the template material over the graph paper. Draw the design exactly as it appears on the graph paper before any cutting is done. This will assure that all the pieces will fit back together properly. Make reference marks.

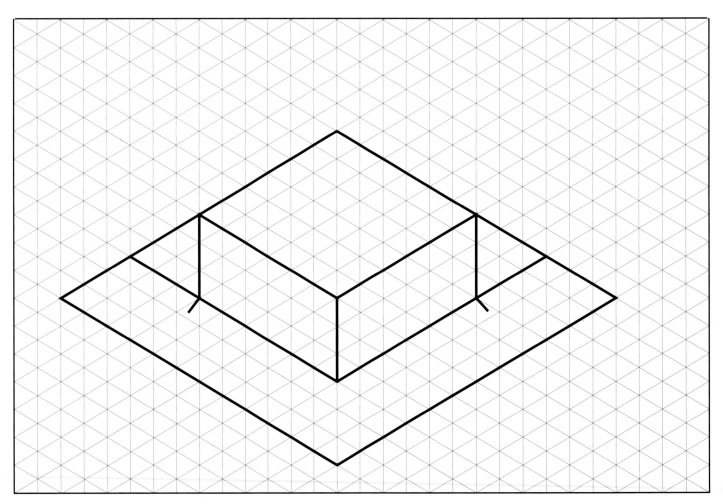

Enlarging

Protractor

If you have a block that is larger than 8" (it will not fit on one sheet of graph paper), you will need to draft it using a ruler and protractor. The angles in isometrics are 60° or 120°.

1. To make a larger template, begin by drawing a vertical line on the template material. Using the proportional wheel, determine how long this line needs to be. Lay the protractor so that its center is on the bottom of this line and the 0 is on the line. Mark 60° from the 0.

2. Make a line through this mark the same length as the vertical line.

3. Lay the protractor at the top of the vertical line and do the same thing, marking 120°. Extend the line the length of the previous lines (all lines will be the same length).

4. A vertical line parallel to the center line will finish the side. If the block is the same on all three sides, break down this diamond into the pieces needed. Draft all three sides in the above manner if the block is different on the sides (as in Slices).

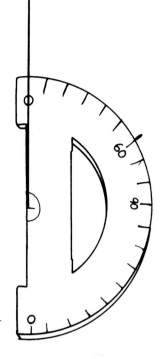

1.

2.

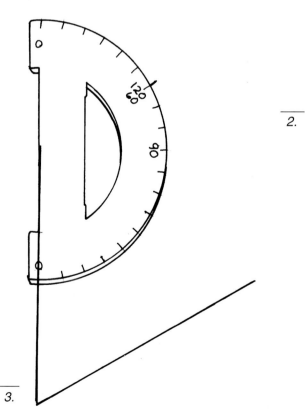

3.

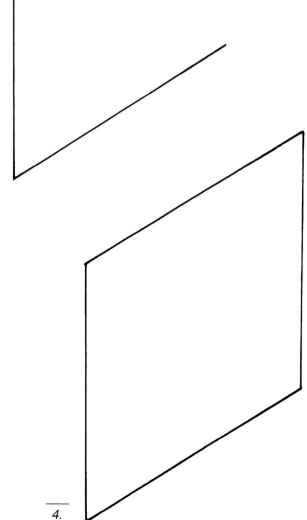

4.

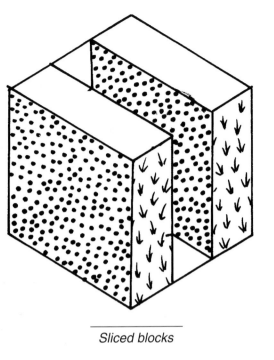

Sliced blocks

Enlarging

Reference Marks

These aid in correct placement of pieces. They are needed anywhere that a seam intersects with another. Mark these carefully onto the template. These references will be transferred to the fabric when you draw the sewing line. They will be seen as little lines in the seam allowance.

Marking

To insure proper marking and cutting, place the template on the pattern in its proper position, then turn the template upside down on the back of the fabric and carefully draw around the template. Be sure to mark all corners clearly. Transfer any reference marks onto the fabric. Cut out the fabric by eyeballing a ¼" seam allowance (this is the same if you are hand or machine piecing). A pin will connect the seam to the mark when you sew.

The template is placed upside down on the back of the fabric; sewing line is marked.

Eyeball cutting a ¼" seam allowance

Color

In each lesson, I have shaded the block with light, medium, and dark. If you look at the Baby Block quilt (plate 1), you will notice that the top of the block is light, one side is medium, and the other side is dark. That holds true for any isometric pattern. To make the pattern as dimensional as possible, a light source must be selected. Generally the light comes from above. The tops of the blocks would all be light. Group your fabrics in this manner: light, medium, and dark.

Blacks

The background for *His* (plate 36) and *Labyrinth* (plate 3) is Iso's, done in varying degrees of black. I grouped all of my black fabrics with small bits of white pattern on them in the light category; lamé was part of this group. The mediums have blacks with little bits of color in them. The darks are made up of black-on-black prints and solid blacks. This method gives a subtle difference between the three surfaces of the Iso's.
Once these were cut using the different templates, I placed them in five different zip-lock bags labeled template B light, template B medium, template C light, C medium, and A dark (refer to Iso's template page 72). Because these are randomly placed, I could sit with my bags, pull one piece from each bag and piece the block.

Black, White and Gray

Iso's 1 (plate 11) is made up of blacks, whites, and grays. I laid my fabrics out from white through gray to black. Working with these fabrics, I started with white in the left top corner, shading to medium gray at the lower right corner. The medium side starts with medium gray and shades to a very dark gray. The dark side is all black.

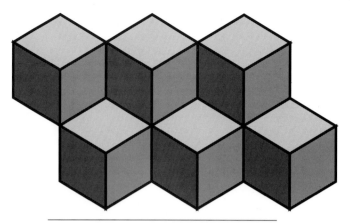

Baby Blocks—light, medium and dark

Light blacks with white

Dark black on black

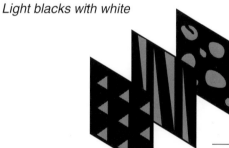

Medium black with bits of color

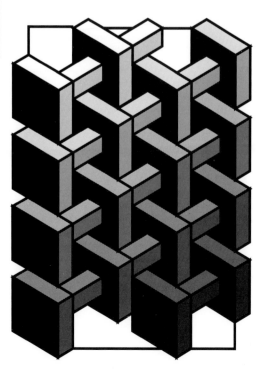

A gradation from light to dark

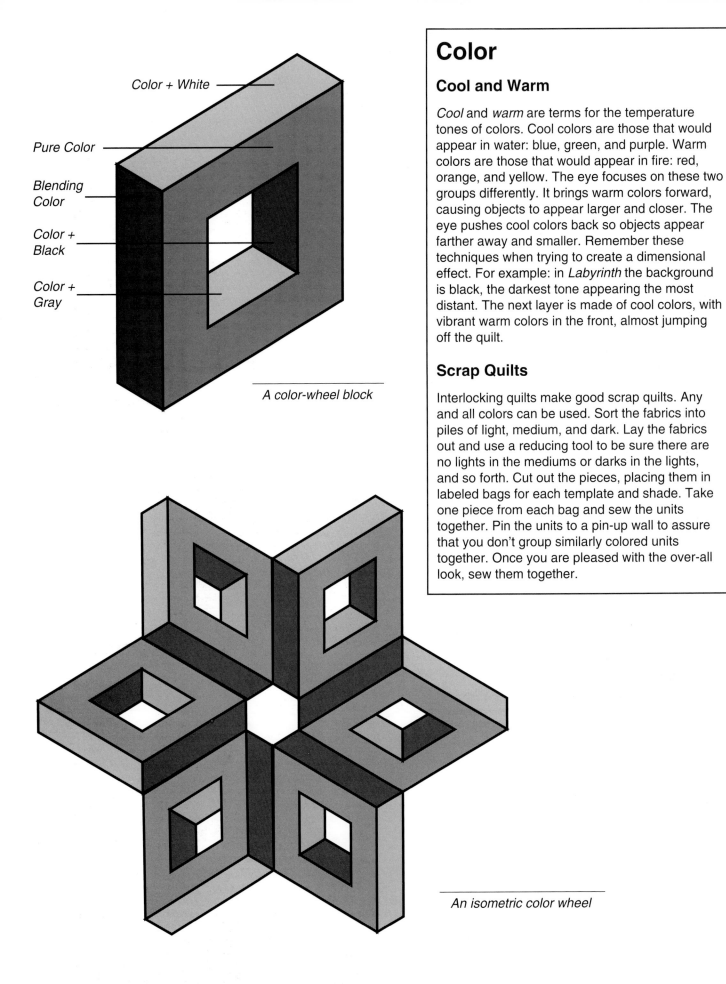

Color + White

Pure Color

Blending Color

Color + Black

Color + Gray

A color-wheel block

An isometric color wheel

Color

Cool and Warm

Cool and *warm* are terms for the temperature tones of colors. Cool colors are those that would appear in water: blue, green, and purple. Warm colors are those that would appear in fire: red, orange, and yellow. The eye focuses on these two groups differently. It brings warm colors forward, causing objects to appear larger and closer. The eye pushes cool colors back so objects appear farther away and smaller. Remember these techniques when trying to create a dimensional effect. For example: in *Labyrinth* the background is black, the darkest tone appearing the most distant. The next layer is made of cool colors, with vibrant warm colors in the front, almost jumping off the quilt.

Scrap Quilts

Interlocking quilts make good scrap quilts. Any and all colors can be used. Sort the fabrics into piles of light, medium, and dark. Lay the fabrics out and use a reducing tool to be sure there are no lights in the mediums or darks in the lights, and so forth. Cut out the pieces, placing them in labeled bags for each template and shade. Take one piece from each bag and sew the units together. Pin the units to a pin-up wall to assure that you don't group similarly colored units together. Once you are pleased with the over-all look, sew them together.

Color

Choices

There are several ways to plan the colors of your quilt. Some artists prefer to color in their drawing with colored pencils or water colors. Others cut actual snippets of fabric and paste them directly onto the drawing. I prefer to work directly on the wall. This enables the drawing and the actual fabrics to guide me in my choices. As I am making my templates, I am thinking about where I want the light source, what elements I want to stand out or to recede, and where the focal point will be. I usually decide on the background first. For me, this is usually black or white. I then begin cutting out the individual pieces, using the templates, marking and cutting accurately and pinning them in place on the pin-up wall. I choose where the warm colors will be next. They will stand out the most and are generally in the front. Once these are cut and pinned to the wall, I stand back and let those chosen colors help me decide the next set. The cool colors are then cut and pinned up.

I notice that my students are often indecisive at the beginning of this pinning-up stage. One or two pieces will be pinned to the wall and they are struggling with whether or not these are right. I will admit that at times I find myself in the same posi-tion. It is necessary to go with the flow and pin many pieces to the wall before being too critical. After all, it is only fabric; once it is all pinned up, it takes no effort to remove a piece and try some-thing else. You will find that the piece or pieces you were unsure of at the beginning will probably blend in perfectly in the end. This is because each piece pinned to the wall affects the choice of the next color.

Another important factor is the difference in value between the layers or even between the different blocks. Use the reducing tool to determine if there is enough value change. Value is the amount of color in a given piece. True, the colors near the light source will need to be light, but if it all washes out through the glass then it will be washed out when the quilt is finished. If this happens, change the front layer to a lighter grouping of colors so there will be a value change. The same process will hold true for each step away from the light source. There needs to be a definite difference between the layers.

Drawing

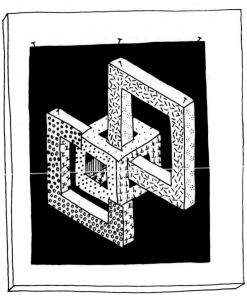

Background fabric pinned to the wall

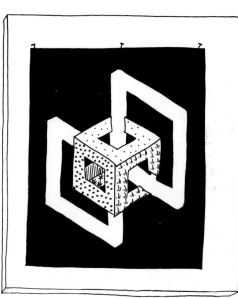

Middle layer pinned in place

A reducing tool is helpful to check color choices once all pieces are pinned to the wall.

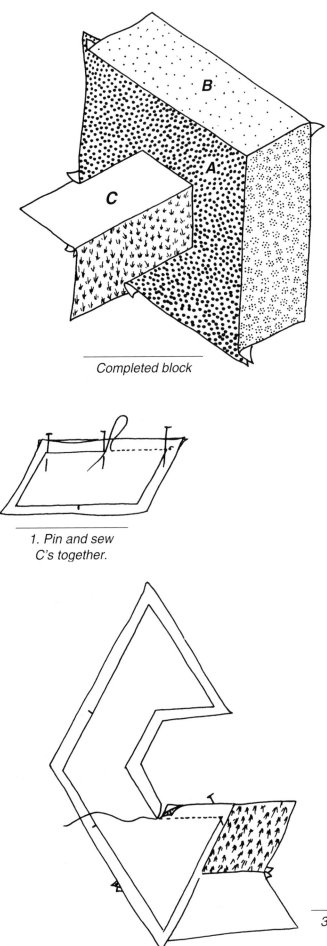

Completed block

Piecing

Iso's is a good place to start to familiarize yourself with piecing isometric units.

There is a pattern on page 72. Make your templates and cut one dark of A, one light and a reverse in medium of B and C. Mark the sewing line on the wrong side of the fabric, eyeball a ¼" seam allowance, and cut.

This is the method for both hand and machine piecing.

1. Sew the C's together on the unmarked side, pinning ends and center and making certain the sewing lines match.

2. Place the reference mark of the medium C on the corner of A and pin. Pin C's corner to A's inside corner.

3. Turn the whole thing over and begin sewing right to left until you reach the corner. Clip into the inside corner of A only, allowing A to turn.

1. Pin and sew C's together.

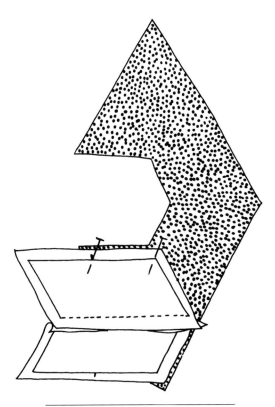

2. Pin C's to first section of A.

3. Sew seam, clip A at inside corner.

Piecing

4. Pin the next corner and sew. Again, clip the corner.

5. Turn, pin, and sew to the corner. Repeat the process for the last side. Finger press.

6. Pin medium B to the side of A and sew.

7. Pin light B in place and sew to the end.

8. Pin the two ends together and sew; press. When you have many units pieced and wish to sew them together, you will need to work diagonally starting at the lower right corner (directions on page 74).

Machine piecing

Many isometric designs can be machine pieced. I prefer to hand piece if the size of the unit is smaller than 4" per side (it seems to be just as fast because the seams are so small). Follow the instructions for hand piecing. Pin ends and centers, being sure sewing line matches up. After a seam is sewn, take the fabric out of the machine to clip the inside corners. Being careful to move all of the fabric out of the way, sew the next seam on the machine.

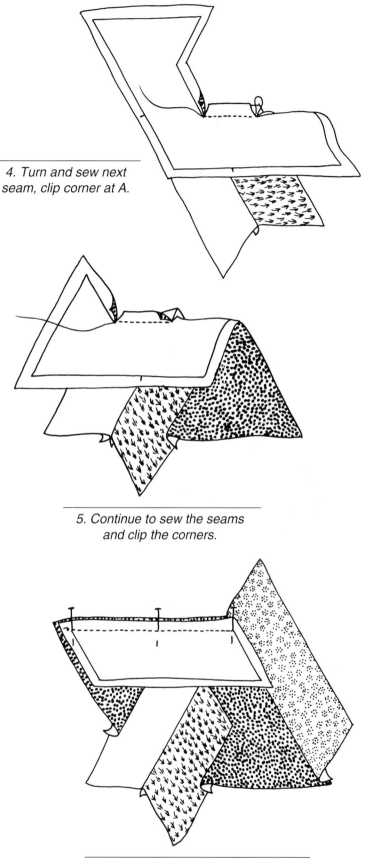

4. Turn and sew next seam, clip corner at A.

5. Continue to sew the seams and clip the corners.

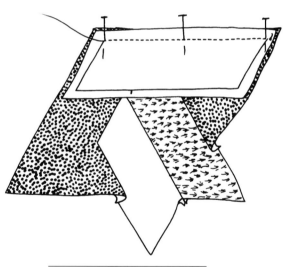

6. Pin and sew medium B to right side of A.

7. Pin light B to top side of A and sew.

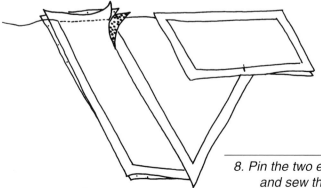

8. Pin the two ends of B together and sew the final seam.

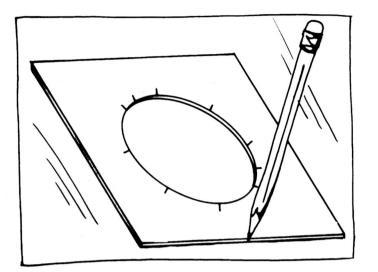

Use template to mark freezer paper.

Pressing

Ellipse

Before appliquéing, you must press the edges under. For ellipses, the freezer paper method gives a smooth edge. Trace around the ellipse template on freezer paper. Cut the freezer paper carefully on the line. Turn the ellipse fabric wrong side up, then lay the waxed side of the freezer paper up on the center of the fabric, matching the edge of the paper with the sewing lines marked on the fabric. With a hot iron, press the ¼" ellipse seam allowance onto the paper. The heat should melt the wax and hold the fabric in place long enough to sew. Lay the ellipse template on the right side of the fabric and lightly transfer the reference marks to the very edge of the ellipse.

Now the inside edge of the ellipse can be put in place. If the background is a solid piece, sew the inside edge of the ellipse and the background together. If the block will be placed over a pieced background, sew the inside edge of the ellipse in place. Do that by first pressing the free edge onto freezer paper. Transfer reference marks to the right side. Place the ellipse edge under the ellipse and pin. Matching these marks, reverse appliqué in place. Remove the freezer paper once everything is sewn in place.

Lay the waxed side of the freezer paper up on back of the fabric and press edge over.

Pin ellipse edge in place.

Appliqué

Hand Appliqué

This is done by pressing the edges of the top piece under and securing it to the bottom piece with a series of small blind stitches. Begin with the needle coming from behind through the edge of the piece being appliquéd. Bring the needle down through the back fabric, being sure to pierce the fabric next to the previous stitch. Come back up a short distance away, through the edge of the piece on top, then back down next to that stitch. Continue on, keeping the stitches small and hidden

Machine Appliqué

This is done by pressing the edges of the top piece under and securing it to the bottom piece using the blind hem stitch on the sewing machine. This method is especially helpful in securing the edges of the different sections in the layered quilts (*Labyrinth*, *Secret Garden*, *Glacier*). Set the sewing machine to blind stitch. This is where the needle will make several stitches on the straight, then take one stitch over to the right or left (depending on the machine), then back to several straight stitches. Use transparent thread on the top and a neutral or matching thread in the bobbin. Set the length and bite as small as possible. Stitch on the base fabric, close to the edge of the piece being appliquéd. The bite should go through close to the edge of the appliquéd piece.

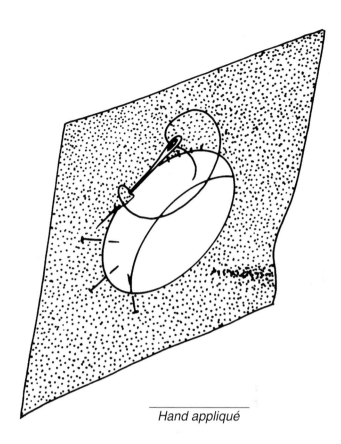

Hand appliqué

Machine appliqué, using the blind hem stitch.

Appliqué

Once the blocks are pieced together, they will need to be appliquéd over the background. All of the free edges need to be pressed under. A pressing template is needed. Cut a piece of lightweight cardboard or matt board at least as big as the largest block in the piece. Make sure that one side is perfectly straight. Lay the straight edge on the wrong side of the fabric, over the drawn sewing line. Roll the fabric over the straight edge with the iron, and press. Do this around all of the free edges of the quilt. To miter corners, lay the pressing template over the next drawn line, fold the corner down along the edge of the template, and press. Using the iron, roll that seam allowance over the pressing template, taking care to keep the corner in position. All raw edges will be hidden.

Use a pressing template to press outside edges under.

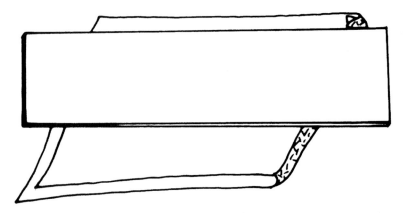

Miter corner by folding point in along pressing template.

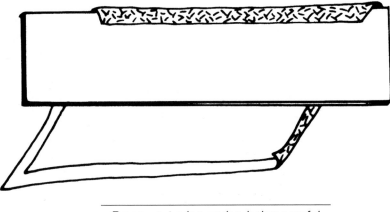

Press next edge under, being careful to keep corner in place.

Putting it Together

The multi-layered quilt can be put together two ways, depending on the number of pieces in the background.

Appliqué: The background layer usually consists of several pieces making up the blocks and many blocks filling the space. Some of the these will not be seen because the front design will overlap and cover them. To save time and fabric, make a template of a complete block. Cut this shape with the ¼" seam allowance out of a color similar to the background. Refer to the drawing to determine how many units will actually show from behind the foreground. Anywhere the unit will not be visible, place a solid piece. This will allow the quilt to hang square and make it easier to appliqué the foreground in place.

Piece together the next layer. Once this is done, press under the outside edges and prepare to appliqué. Pin the foreground over the pieced background on the pin-up wall. It is important that all of the vertical lines are indeed vertical. Pin a length of string to the wall above the quilt and tie a spool of thread to the other end. This gives a true vertical line. Check to make sure that the vertical lines of the blocks are parallel to the string. I pin the string further along the top of the quilt, checking the verticals at various points.

When you are sure that everything is straight, baste the layers together so you can take the fabric off the wall. Appliqué all the layers together. This can be done by hand or by machine. Upon completing the appliqué, turn the quilt over and trim away parts of blocks that are behind others, leaving only one layer through which to quilt.

This method was used for *Labyrinth* and *Wedding Quilt*.

Background layer with solid blocks where front layer will cover

Front layer of Wedding Quilt

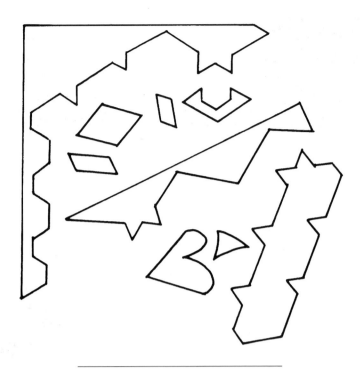

Templates cut apart for marking

Putting it Together

Another way to complete the multi-layered quilt is to piece the layers together. This is the easiest way if there are not many pieces in the background.

Machine piecing: In this method, you construct only as much background as will be seen. The background ends where the foreground begins. The entire design is drawn on the matt board and each piece is cut out and used as a separate template. If there are many identical templates, a master may be made. The matt board templates would be used only where they differ from the master template (where they end at a foreground piece). Once the background is completed, it is pieced to the foreground as they come into contact. There will be many corners to deal with. Remember to release the corners by clipping the inside points. Match reference marks and pin accurately.

This method was used for *Dimensional Portal* and *Bearding Pedestrian*.

Bearding Pedestrian
*drawing on
matt board*

Free Form

Glacier and *Secret Garden*

A freer method was used to design this quilt than has been previously described. I started with a photograph of a magnificent Alaskan glacier. I studied the photo, getting acquainted with the lights and darks, the flow of the river of ice, and the mountains. I drew a very sketchy guide interpreting these elements as different isometric blocks. For instance, the fresh snow on top was going to be small Baby Blocks all in white. I made the template, cut out the whites, pieced each block, then pinned them across the top of my pin-up wall. The mountain was next. I made the Rocks template, cut out the brown fabrics, sewed each block, then pinned them to the wall. The glacier itself was interpreted with many different isometric blocks. All of these were pinned up within their groupings. I continued in this manner until the glacier was completed. This was a little scary because I am used to working with a completed drawing, knowing what the final piece will look like. It was also very exciting because I was creating as I was going, each part dictating what I did next. Once the whole thing was pinned up, it was time to sew the sections together. I started with the mountain, sewing all of the Rock blocks together to create one large grouping. Then I moved on to the fresh snow of Baby Blocks, sewing them together as one, continuing with all of the groupings until all were sewn together. The groupings were then pinned on the wall, with the verticals of all the different groupings parallel. They were then basted together, taken to the wall and appliquéd together.

The same method was followed for *My Secret Garden*. This one was inspired by a photo of a garden. Again, a rough sketch set the stage for the isometric blocks.

Two end photos of an Alaskan glacier

Rough sketch for Glacier *quilt*

Rough sketch for My Secret Garden *quilt*

Photo of a garden

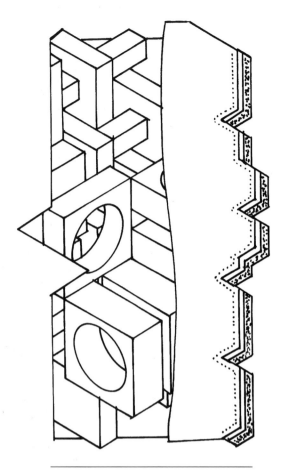

Sew facing to front edge of quilt.

Finishing

There are two ways to finish the outside edges of the quilt. For a straight-edged quilt, the best way is to use bias binding. To make this binding, fold the fabric on the diagonal, making sure the edges match; press. The fold is the 45° angle known as the bias; cut 1¾" strips from the fold. Sew as many lengths together as needed. Press in half lengthwise with the wrong sides together. Machine stitch the bias to the front of the quilt, turn it to the back and hand stitch it in place.

Many times the design of the quilt breaks through the outside edges, creating a more interesting edge. Using a facing to finish the piece is more effective. Take strips of fabric the same length as the edge of the quilt. Trim the batting and backing to the edge. Baste one length of the facing, right sides together, to one side of the quilt. Trim the facing to match the quilt edge. With the facing on the top, stitch ¼" from the edge. Be sure to pivot exactly at the corners so the integrity of each piece is kept intact. When you are about an inch from a pivot point, lift the facing up and find the corner; mark that spot on the facing so you know exactly where to turn. Sew to the mark; with the needle in the down position, lift the foot, turn the quilt, and sew to the next corner. Complete the other sides in the same manner.

Trim the seam allowance and carefully clip into each inside corner. Turn the facing to the back. Pull out each corner and point. Press lightly. Turn the raw edge in and hand sew in place. Miter corners.

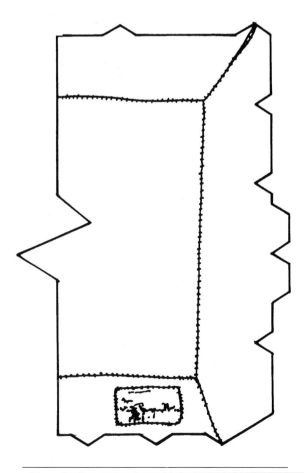

Turn facing to back and blind stitch in place.

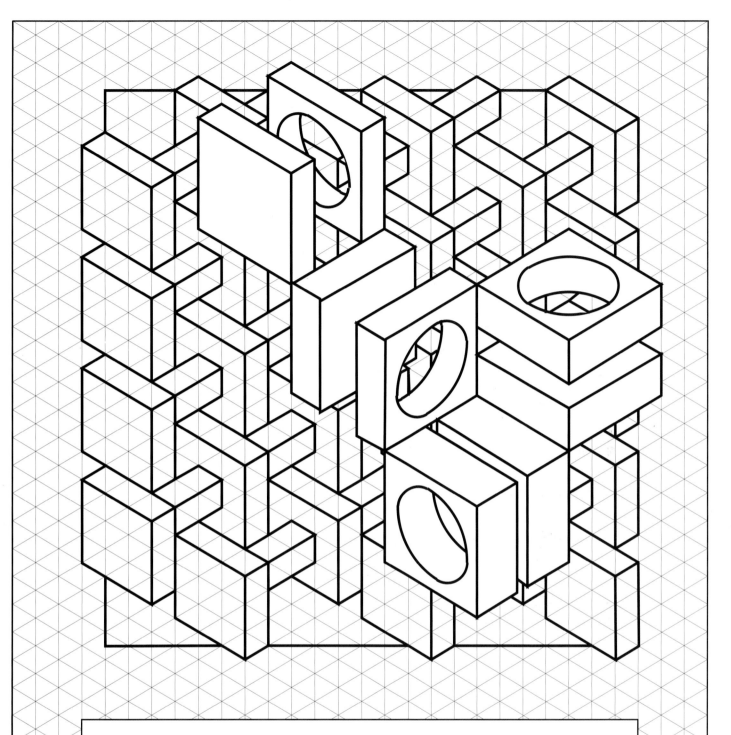

Pattern: Nuts and Bolts

The accurate templates and directions are on the following pages. Make the templates as they are shown; do not add a seam allowance. This pattern can be used for machine or hand piecing.

Fabrics: Background—At least ten different lights, mediums, and darks, in whatever colors you prefer. Several different possibilities are shown on page 48 of the color section. Select a variety from your fabric collection. Front blocks—Choose a different grouping of colors in a variety of lights, mediums, and darks. If you must purchase fabric, a quarter yard would be enough of each of many different pieces.

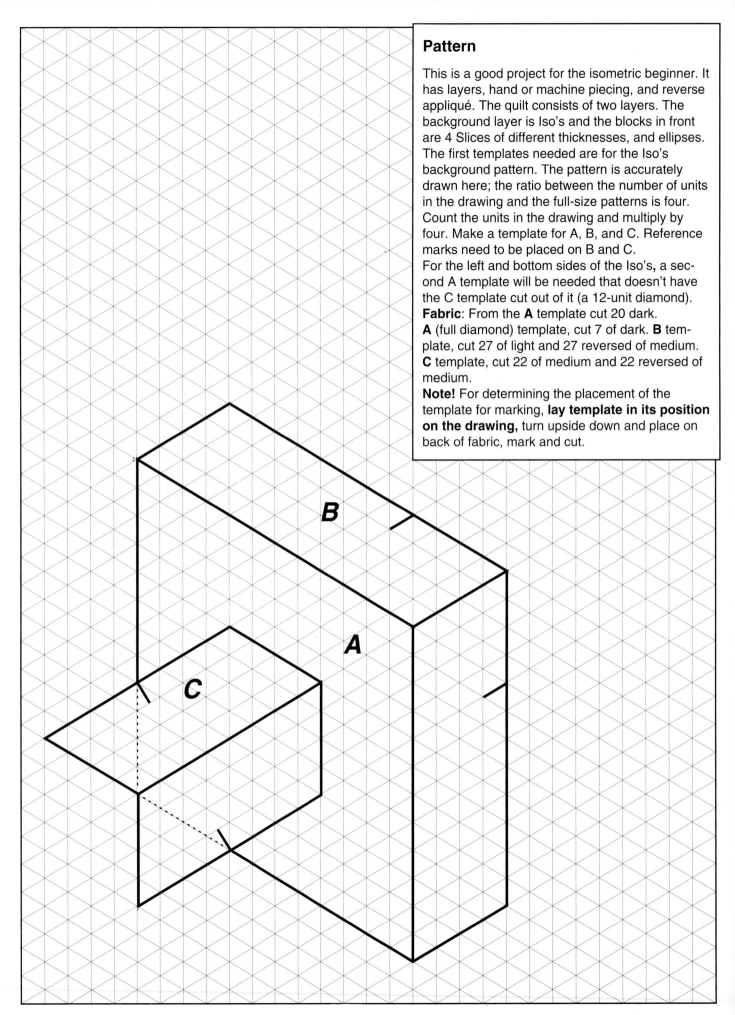

Pattern

This is a good project for the isometric beginner. It has layers, hand or machine piecing, and reverse appliqué. The quilt consists of two layers. The background layer is Iso's and the blocks in front are 4 Slices of different thicknesses, and ellipses. The first templates needed are for the Iso's background pattern. The pattern is accurately drawn here; the ratio between the number of units in the drawing and the full-size patterns is four. Count the units in the drawing and multiply by four. Make a template for A, B, and C. Reference marks need to be placed on B and C.

For the left and bottom sides of the Iso's, a second A template will be needed that doesn't have the C template cut out of it (a 12-unit diamond).

Fabric: From the **A** template cut 20 dark.
A (full diamond) template, cut 7 of dark. **B** template, cut 27 of light and 27 reversed of medium. **C** template, cut 22 of medium and 22 reversed of medium.

Note! For determining the placement of the template for marking, **lay template in its position on the drawing,** turn upside down and place on back of fabric, mark and cut.

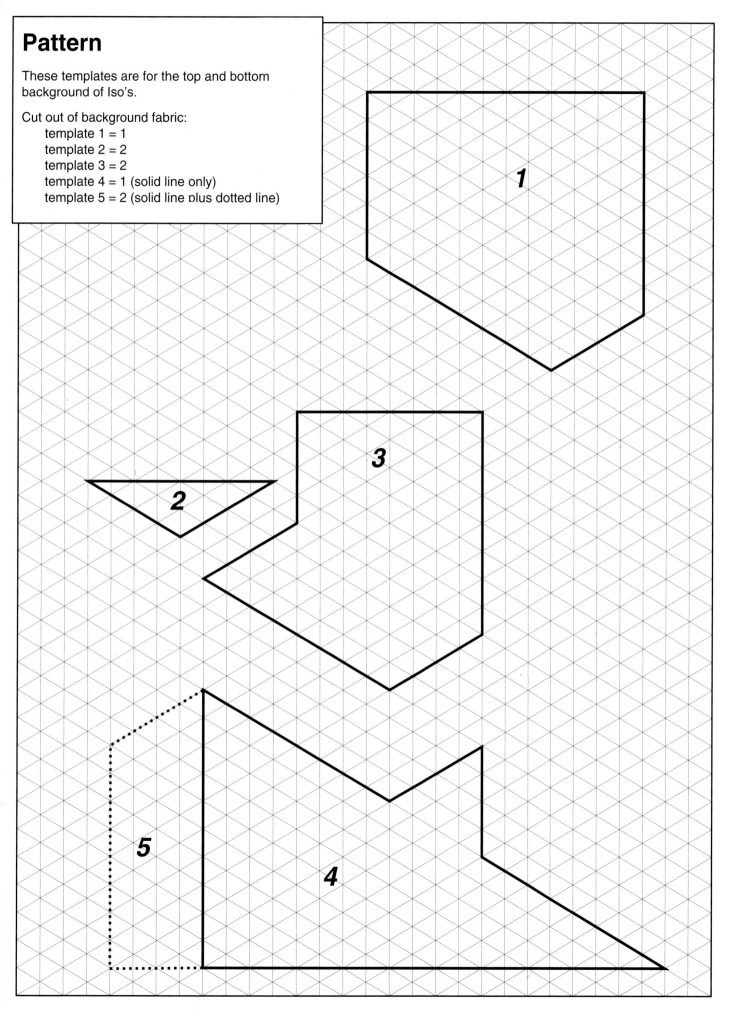

Pattern

These templates are for the top and bottom background of Iso's.

Cut out of background fabric:
    template 1 = 1
    template 2 = 2
    template 3 = 2
    template 4 = 1 (solid line only)
    template 5 = 2 (solid line plus dotted line)

1

3

2

5

4

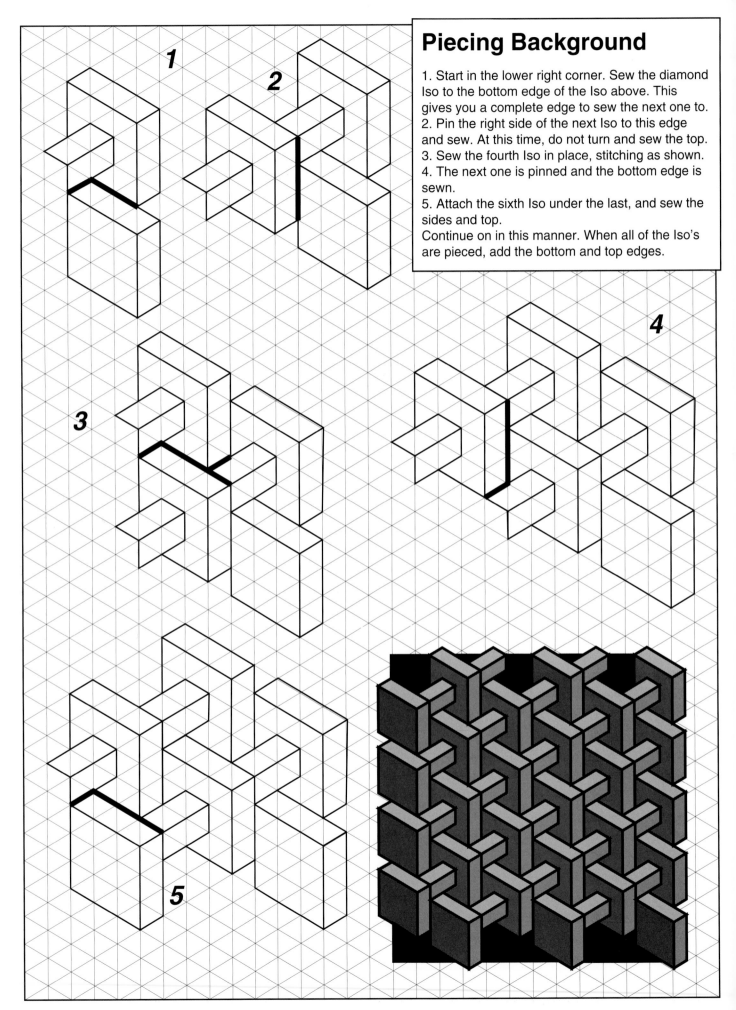

Piecing Background

1. Start in the lower right corner. Sew the diamond Iso to the bottom edge of the Iso above. This gives you a complete edge to sew the next one to.
2. Pin the right side of the next Iso to this edge and sew. At this time, do not turn and sew the top.
3. Sew the fourth Iso in place, stitching as shown.
4. The next one is pinned and the bottom edge is sewn.
5. Attach the sixth Iso under the last, and sew the sides and top.
Continue on in this manner. When all of the Iso's are pieced, add the bottom and top edges.

Piecing the Top Layer

The top layer is made of Slices with ellipses.

Block 1 **Templates**

Edge: cut 2 light and 2 medium (The two reference marks are only on the front slice for placement of the back slice).
Diamond (without ellipse): cut 1 dark.
Ellipse: cut 1 dark.
Ellipse edge: cut 1 medium dark.
Remember to place the template upside down on the back of the fabric.

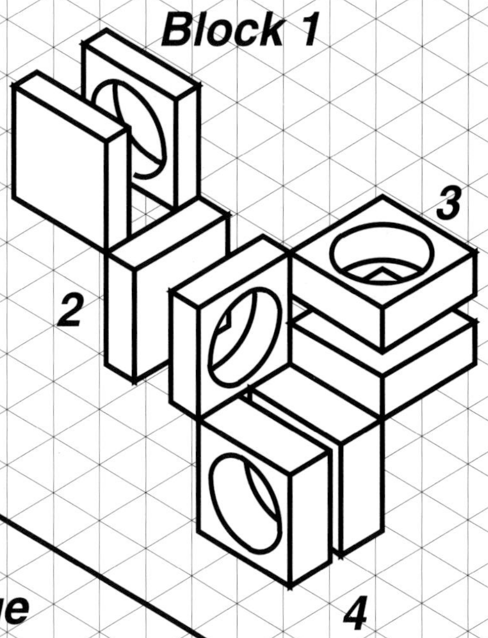

Block 1

2

3

4

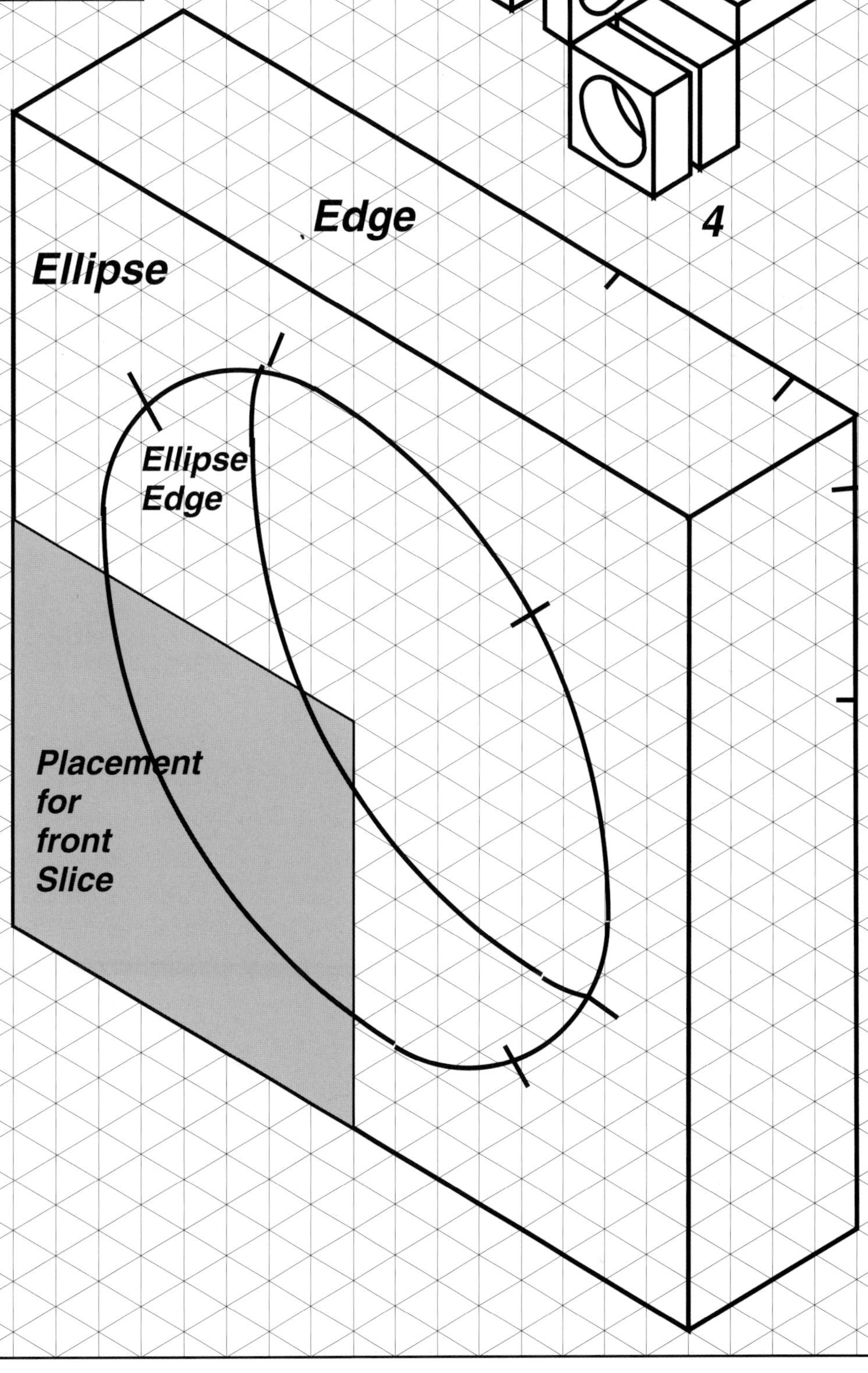

Edge

Ellipse

Ellipse Edge

Placement for front Slice

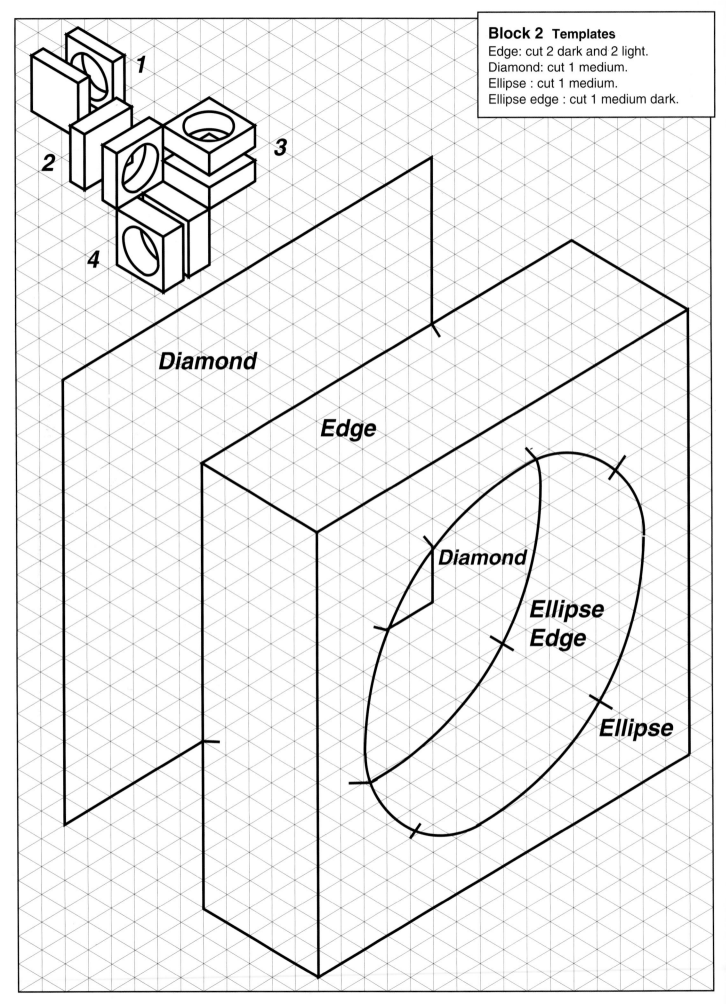

Block 2 Templates
Edge: cut 2 dark and 2 light.
Diamond: cut 1 medium.
Ellipse : cut 1 medium.
Ellipse edge : cut 1 medium dark.

Diamond

Edge

Diamond

Ellipse Edge

Ellipse

Block 3 Templates
Edge: cut 2 dark and 2 medium.
Diamond: cut 1 light.
Ellipse: cut 1 light.
Ellipse edge: cut 1 medium.

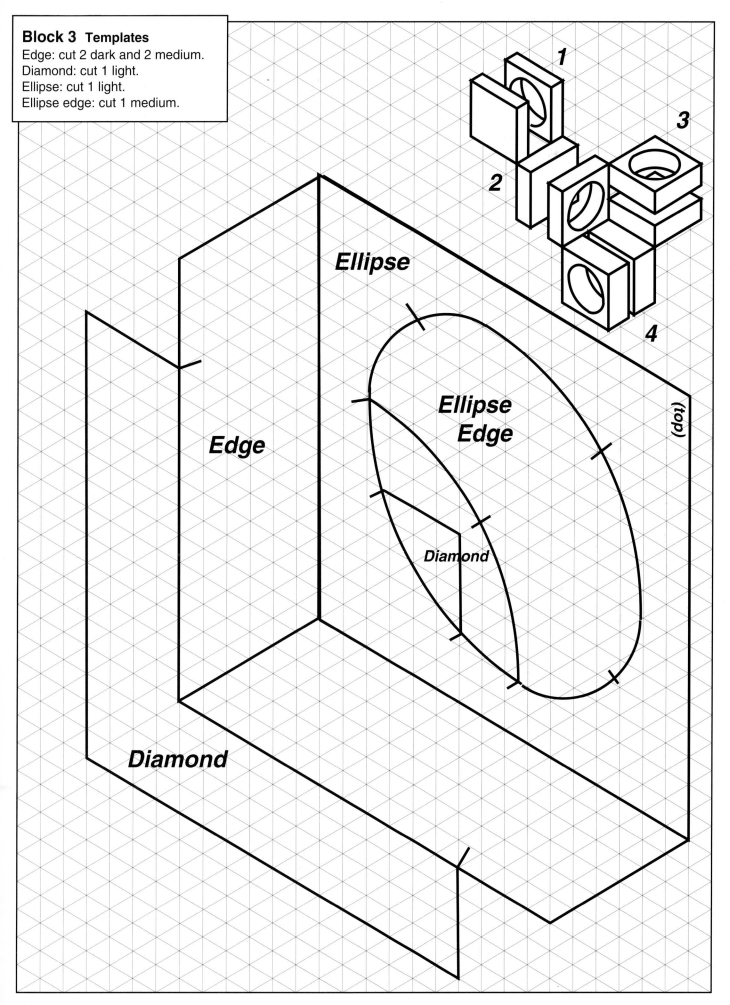

1

3

2

4

Ellipse

Edge

Ellipse
Edge

(top)

Diamond

Diamond

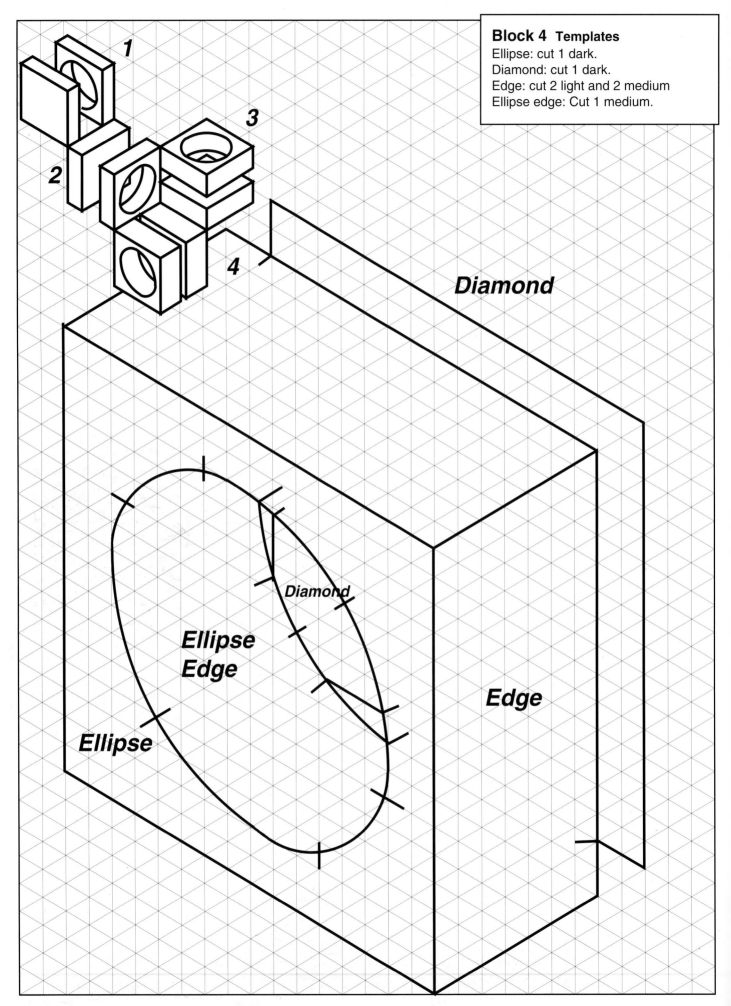

Block 4 Templates
Ellipse: cut 1 dark.
Diamond: cut 1 dark.
Edge: cut 2 light and 2 medium
Ellipse edge: Cut 1 medium.

1

2

3

4

Diamond

Diamond

Ellipse Edge

Ellipse

Edge

Pattern

Piece the blocks together. Machine or hand piece the straight seams and reverse appliqué the ellipses. Once the ellipse has been pressed under onto the freezer paper, place the inside of the hole in position, matching reference marks. Appliqué that part in place. If the opening shows the corner of the under slice, put that in place and appliqué that portion, being sure to leave the seam allowance open. Leave the freezer paper in place until the blocks have been sewn onto the background.

Piece the blocks together; be sure to pin reference marks and sew only between these marks, leaving the seam allowance open.

Press all free edges under on the sewing line. Refer to pressing instructions on page 66. Place all 4 blocks as one unit over the Iso's background (if you prefer, these could be placed over a solid background). Make sure all vertical lines are vertical, either by using a plumb bob or by measuring from the outside edge. Machine or hand appliqué in place. Turn the piece over and carefully trim the background out from behind the foreground blocks.

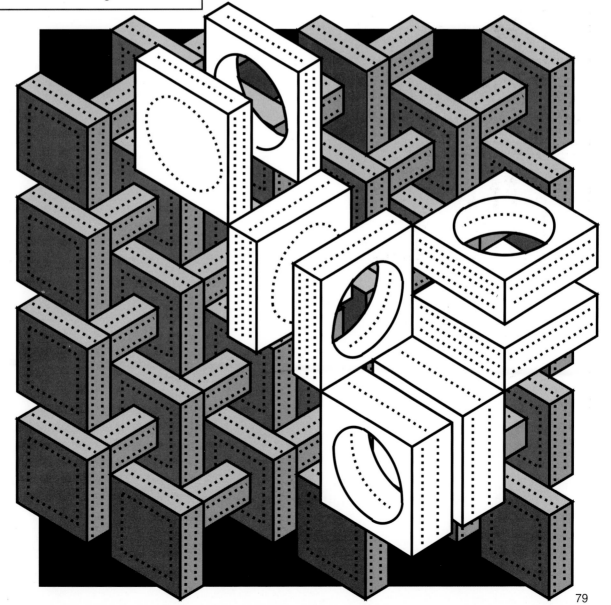

Other Books by Katie

3 Dimensional Design

Mandala

For additional tools, supplies, and fabrics, send SASE to:

*Katie Pasquini-Masopust
230 Rancho Alegre Rd.
Santa Fe, NM 87505*

Other Fine Quilting Books from C&T Publishing

An Amish Adventure, Roberta Horton

Appliqué 12 Easy Ways!, Elly Sienkiewicz

The Art of Silk Ribbon Embroidery, Judith Montano

Baltimore Album Quilts, Historic Notes and Antique Patterns, Elly Sienkiewicz

Baltimore Beauties and Beyond (2 Volumes), Elly Sienkiewicz

The Boston Commons Quilt, Blanche Young and Helen Young Frost

Calico and Beyond, Roberta Horton

A Celebration of Hearts, Jean Wells and Marina Anderson

Christmas Traditions from the Heart, Margaret Peters

Crazy Quilt Handbook, Judith Montano

Crazy Quilt Odyssey, Judith Montano

Design a Baltimore Album Quilt!, Elly Sienkiewicz

Fans, Jean Wells

Fine Feathers, Marianne Fons

The Flying Geese Quilt, Blanche Young and Helen Young Frost

Friendship's Offering, Susan McKelvey

Happy Trails, Pepper Cory

Heirloom Machine Quilting, Harriet Hargrave

Imagery on Fabric, Jean Ray Laury

The Irish Chain Quilt, Blanche Young and Helen Young Frost

Landscapes & Illusions, Joen Wolfrom

Let's Make Waves, Marianne Fons and Liz Porter

Light and Shadows, Susan McKelvey

The Magical Effects of Color, Joen Wolfrom

Mariner's Compass, Judy Mathieson

Mastering Machine Appliqué, Harriet Hargrave

Memorabilia Quilting, Jean Wells

The New Lone Star Handbook, Blanche Young and Helen Young Frost

Perfect Pineapples, Jane Hall and Dixie Haywood

Picture This, Jean Wells and Marina Anderson

Plaids and Stripes, Roberta Horton

Patchwork Quilts Made Easy (PQME) Series: Milky Way Quilt, Jean Wells

PQME Series: Nine-Patch Quilt, Jean Wells

PQME Series: Pinwheel Quilt, Jean Wells

PQME Series: Stars & Hearts Quilt, Jean Wells

Quilting Designs from Antique Quilts, Pepper Cory

Quilting Designs from the Amish, Pepper Cory

Story Quilts, Mary Mashuta

Trip Around the World Quilts, Blanche Young and Helen Young Frost

Visions: The Art of the Quilt, Quilt San Diego

Visions: Quilts of a New Decade, Quilt San Diego

Working in Miniature, Becky Schaefer

Wearable Art for Real People, Mary Mashuta

For a complete listing of fine quilting books from C&T Publishing, write for a free catalog:

C&T Publishing
P.O. Box 1456
Lafayette, CA 94549
800-284-1114